More Praise for *Co-Teaching That Works*

"Co-teaching is a reality in today's schools. Classroom teachers and specialists of all kinds will appreciate the great variety of co-teaching models to explore and adapt to their own settings. The many examples of co-taught lessons and co-teaching tips are clearly laid out to encourage teaching teams to try them out."

—**Sylvia Sklar,** assistant professor and associate director, Centre for Educational Leadership, McGill University

"Anne Beninghof has so much to share with administrators and teachers on maximizing the benefits of co-teaching. That's because she lives it! Anne guides teachers in 'real' classrooms so that structures and strategies are intentional and produce achievement results for kids."

—**Jane Byers,** Director of Special Services, Papillion-La Vista School District, Papillion, NE

Jossey-Bass Teacher

Jossey-Bass Teacher provides educators with practical knowledge and tools to create a positive and lifelong impact on student learning. We offer classroom-tested and research-based teaching resources for a variety of grade levels and subject areas. Whether you are an aspiring, new, or veteran teacher, we want to help you make every teaching day your best.

From ready-to-use classroom activities to the latest teaching framework, our value-packed books provide insightful, practical, and comprehensive materials on the topics that matter most to K–12 teachers. We hope to become your trusted source for the best ideas from the most experienced and respected experts in the field.

Co-Teaching That Works
Structures and Strategies for Maximizing Student Learning

Anne M. Beninghof

JOSSEY-BASS
A Wiley Imprint
www.josseybass.com

Published by Jossey-Bass
A Wiley Imprint
One Montgomery Street, Suite 1200, San Francisco, CA 94104-4594—www.josseybass.com

Jossey-Bass books and products are available through most bookstores. To contact Jossey-Bass directly call
our Customer Care Department within the U.S. at 800-956-7739, outside the U.S. at 317-572-3986, or fax
317-572-4002.

Wiley publishes in a variety of print and electronic formats and by print-on-demand. Some material
included with standard print versions of this book may not be included in e-books or in print-on-demand. If
this book refers to
media such as a CD or DVD that is not included in the version you purchased, you may download this
material at **http://booksupport.wiley.com**. For more information about Wiley products, visit **www.wiley.com**.

Library of Congress Cataloging-in-Publication Data
Beninghof, Anne M.
    Co-teaching that works : structures and strategies for maximizing student learning / Anne M. Beninghof.
– 1st ed.
        p. cm.
    Includes bibliographical references and index.
    ISBN 978-1-118-00436-4 (pbk.), ISBN 978-1-118-18041-9 (ebk.), ISBN 978-1-118-18042-6 (ebk.), ISBN 978-1-118-
18043-3 (ebk.)
1. Teaching teams.   2. Classroom management.   I. Title.
    LB1029.T4B46 2012
    371.14'8–dc23

                                    2011039115

Printed in the United States of America
FIRST EDITION
PB Printing   10 9 8 7

THE AUTHOR

Anne M. Beninghof, an internationally recognized consultant and trainer, has more than thirty years of experience working with students and teachers in a variety of public and private settings. She has been a special education teacher, adjunct faculty member of the University of Hartford and the University of Colorado, has published several books and videos, and provided staff development in 49 states. She has also collaborated with numerous state agencies to bring about inclusive practices. Several years ago Anne decided to follow her heart and return to the classroom, where she works part-time with teachers and students who are struggling with the learning process. In both her presenting and writing, Anne focuses on creative, practical solutions for more effectively including students with diverse learning needs in general education classrooms.

Woodrow Wilson once said, "I not only use all of the brains I have, but all I can borrow." Thanks to all of the generous educators and students who let me borrow their brains for the development of this book.

CONTENTS

Co-Teaching That Works

Introduction

When I was only seven, I committed my first crime. My parents had gone out to run errands, leaving my two older brothers in charge. Ensconced in front of the weekly football game on TV, they paid no attention to their little sister. Bored with football, I decided that I had the perfect opportunity to explore my parents' bedroom. My parents, continually harassed by four children, considered their bedroom an oasis, off-limits to us unless by special invitation. Thus, the temptation. I opened the top drawer to my father's walnut dresser and, standing on tiptoes, peered inside to see what treasures it might hold. Tucked into one corner was an uncovered box, filled with shiny coins that he removed from his trouser pockets each night. I quickly snatched a nickel and dropped it into the front pocket of my skirt. Glancing over my shoulder guiltily, I found that the world had not changed one bit, so I continued exploring.

Wedged into the back of the drawer, under some graying, fraying hankies, there was a tube-shaped object, kind of brassy in color. My fingers reached for it, closing around the cool metal and pulling it forward. As I examined it more closely, I found that one end was narrow, with a circle of glass over it, while the other end was wider with a fuzzy bit of glass covering it. I put the narrow end up to my eye to look inside and squealed in delight at the storm of colors that rained down. This of course brought my brothers running. My life of crime was over, but my lifelong love of kaleidoscopes had just begun.

Kaleidoscopes are the perfect metaphor for co-teaching. A kaleidoscope is a tube of mirrors that contains loose beads or small objects that can vary in color and size. By turning the tube, an unlimited number of combinations occur to create unique designs. The colors and shapes shift easily to produce a new picture, a new blending of ingredients. The possibilities are endless. So it is with co-teaching. When two adults work closely together to teach a heterogeneous group of students, the classroom portrait will be unique and ever-changing, based on the students, the curriculum, and the strengths that each person contributes to the picture.

> *When two adults work closely together to teach a heterogeneous group of students, the classroom portrait will be unique and ever-changing.*

For some educators, the kaleidoscope of co-teaching can be intimidating. "What does it look like?" "Who's in charge?" and "Tell me how to do it" are commonly heard requests. Stepping into the unknown world of working closely with another teacher, obliged to teach students with a wide variety of needs, can cause apprehension for new and veteran teachers alike. A detailed step-by-step guide may seem to be the answer.

But effective co-teaching must be recognized as a changing, accommodating, flexible form of teaching in order to be responsive to the needs of the heterogeneous group of students. A lock-step "how-to" manual will not allow for the myriad factors that affect the co-teaching classroom. Instead, loose, flexible frameworks from which you can develop your own unique display of effective instruction work best. These frameworks, or models, describe ways in which two or more adults can work together to co-teach. By examining student factors, the curriculum, and available resources, co-teachers determine which model or models to use for a specific lesson or unit, blending them to create an instructional solution.

Blending all of the instructional factors into the best possible solution requires many decisions. When I worked as a solo teacher, all by myself in my classroom, I had what felt like a thousand decisions to make each day. Of course, there were the big decisions about what and how to teach. But there were lots of other decisions which might have seemed "little." Should I let Mark's sloppy homework slide by because I knew his parents were in divorce proceedings? Could Rachel and Tamlyn work effectively in the same group after the friendship-ending blowup they had yesterday? What color of paper should I use for copying the science worksheet? Enter a co-teacher. Now each of these decisions may require consensus. Now each of these decisions may take more time. Now each of these decisions may be better!

Over time we have learned strategies for making co-teaching decisions more effectively and efficiently (Murawski, 2008; Dieker, 2001). These strategies will be presented throughout this book. We have also learned that certain personal characteristics—flexibility and open-mindedness—lend themselves well to establishing and maintaining strong co-teaching relationships. And perhaps most important, we have learned that individual co-teaching partnerships must design their own unique model of co-teaching to best serve their students. This book will provide you with dozens of practical ideas for making your co-teaching more effective. Whether your partnership includes a special educator, a technology specialist, or an occupational therapist, there are ideas for you. Whether your partnership has abundant planning time or hardly any, there are ideas for you. Whether your instruction is highly differentiated or in the early stages, there are dozens of ideas that will work for you!

Chapter One provides a working definition of co-teaching for the purpose of this book, a review of the benefits and current research. It will lay the groundwork for understanding what co-teaching looks like when described in greater detail throughout the remainder of the book. As you read it, consider the benefits that are most important to you and your partner. What do you hope to accomplish?

Chapters Two and Three explore common challenges experienced by co-teachers and ideas for overcoming them. Solutions include schoolwide efforts as well as teacher-to-teacher possibilities. Many of the ideas presented are proactive and can bring about a positive culture of inclusiveness for the entire learning community. All teachers and students benefit when these attributes of inclusion are present—even if they are not currently involved in co-teaching. As you read these chapters, consider an action plan to incorporate some positive changes.

Part Two includes chapters describing nine models of co-teaching. Each model is described in detail, using Teacher A and Teacher B to refer to the partners. Teacher A is usually the general education teacher, and Teacher B is usually the specialist, but there are also times when it is best to flip-flop the roles. Think flexibly about these as you peruse the examples. Each chapter will contain sample lesson plans, an outline of roles and responsibilities for the two teachers, and pros and cons to consider. Many of the lesson plans include practical instructional strategies, marked with a puzzle piece icon that are explained in detail in the appendix. Be ready to dog-ear pages that seem a good fit for you so that you can quickly find them again.

Part Three contains chapters describing co-teaching with eight different types of specialists. These chapters detail some of the unique characteristics of partnering with a type of specialist, sample lesson plans, and specific advice on actions essential for success. Browse all eight chapters or turn to the one most relevant to you.

Following the conclusion is an appendix filled with "how-to" strategies for many of the innovative instructional strategies included in sample lesson plans. In addition to step-by-step directions for implementation, illustrations and black-line reproducibles are provided so that the ideas can be implemented with ease. You may wish to flip to the appendix when you see an unfamiliar strategy within a lesson plan. Be prepared with sticky notes to flag the strategies you want to use right away!

As you read about the co-teachers who share their stories here, you will see that they have each combined their own strengths, used various structures and strategies, and created their own kaleidoscope picture in order to best serve their students. What will your kaleidoscope look like?

PART ONE

PUTTING TOGETHER
THE PIECES

An Overview of Co-Teaching

What Is Co-Teaching?

Co-teaching (or collaborative teaching) is a coordinated instructional practice in which two or more educators simultaneously work with a heterogeneous group of students in a general education classroom.

Several key terms in this definition emphasize essential elements for success. First, co-teaching is **coordinated**. Co-teaching partners spend time planning together, smoothly share instructional responsibilities, and collaboratively reflect on their practices. Effective co-teaching can be compared to synchronized swimming—teammates must carefully coordinate, not only to win but to avoid drowning!

> *Effective co-teaching can be compared to synchronized swimming—teammates must carefully coordinate, not only to win but to avoid drowning!*

Many different **educators** can be involved in co-teaching relationships. Historically, special education teachers have been the most common to partner with classroom teachers, but this is rapidly changing. Successful partnerships have developed with ELL teachers, speech therapists, librarians, literacy specialists, occupational and physical therapists, gifted specialists, technology specialists, social workers, and school psychologists. Inclusive schools seek innovative ways to use all staff to directly support student learning. In addition, powerful examples exist of co-teaching with paraeducators or instructional aides. Of course, how these individuals co-teach will depend on the expertise they bring to the classroom and the time they have available.

Co-teaching differs from collaborative consultation because both educators are **simultaneously** engaged in the instructional process. Rather than a specialist suggesting a few instructional ideas to a teacher and then retreating, the partners are implementing the planned instruction together. As future chapters will detail, co-teaching can look many different ways to the casual observer. Within one period, we may see both teachers take a lead in lecturing, giving directions, monitoring student behavior, or taking responsibility for a small group. We may see one teacher quietly collecting observational data while the other facilitates whole-group instruction, or one teacher problem solving with an individual student while the other continues the lesson. No matter what it looks like, effective co-teaching always requires the active engagement of both educators for the entire period.

Other definitions of co-teaching exist (Basso and McCoy, 2007; Murawski, 2009; Villa, Thousand, and Nevin, 2004; Fattig and Taylor, 2008.) In a 2009 survey of state education agencies, researchers found quite a number of different definitions.

- Virginia: "Co-teaching means a service delivery option with two or more professionals sharing responsibility for a group of students for some or all of the school day in order to combine their expertise to meet student needs."

- Iowa: "Co-teaching is defined as two teachers physically present in a heterogeneous classroom with joint and equal responsibility for classroom instruction."

- Oklahoma: "Co-teaching implies a partnership in the classroom of a teacher with general education credentials and a special education teacher with special education and/or content credentials. This partnership creates a qualitatively different classroom than one with only a single teacher. A change of instructional intensity is also often noted in the descriptions of this type of classroom that is operated by two teachers and meets the instructional needs of all students in the classroom."

- New York: "Integrated co-teaching services means the provision of specially designed instruction and academic instruction provided to a group of students with disabilities and nondisabled students."

What Does the Research Say?

In fact, so many different definitions and interpretations exist that it has been difficult to gather data on the effectiveness of co-teaching. In somewhat of an understatement, one educator concluded "Co-teaching is not a phenomenon that lends itself to precise investigation" (DLDCEC, 2001).

A small amount of research on co-teaching shows the following results:

- In a study of vocabulary acquisition in primary grades, researchers found that children with speech-language impairments made stronger gains in a co-taught setting (between a classroom teacher and an SLP) than in pull-out or in-class support (Throneburg, 2000).

- A study centered on the infusion of language skills (vocabulary, phonemic awareness) in urban kindergarten settings found that ELL students and native English speakers in a co-taught classroom (classroom teacher and an SLP) showed significantly greater language gains than those in a traditional classroom (Hadley, Simmerman, Long, and Luna, 2000).

- A New York elementary school found literacy achievement increased for students with disabilities, from 20 percent at or above grade level to 42 percent in just two years as a result of co-teaching intervention (Theoharis and Causton-Theoharis, 2010).

- A Georgia middle school found that students with and without disabilities showed significant increases on standardized tests in mathematics and language arts after two years of co-teaching. In addition, there was a significant decrease in the numbers of students with chronic attendance problems (Burns, 2010).

- Meta-analyses of the research on co-teaching with special educators found only a handful of well-designed studies to include in the review. The results of these studies indicated that co-teaching may be moderately effective in language arts and mathematics (Murawski and Swanson, 2001; Scruggs, Mastropieri and McDuffe, 2007).

While the available research shows positive results associated with co-teaching, the current database is extremely limited. As co-teaching becomes a growing response to student needs and federal mandates, educators hope that the research base will also continue to grow.

What Are the Benefits?

The good news is that many practicing educators report positive outcomes from co-teaching. Observed benefits include:

- Professional Growth: Undergraduate programs can only pack so much into a four-year plan. Classroom teachers and specialists begin their jobs, understandably, with a limited knowledge and experience base. If they work in isolation, that knowledge and experience base will continue to have limits. In contrast, educators who co-teach have the opportunity to learn from daily interaction and observation of a colleague with a very different background. For specialists, on the one hand, this usually means deepening and broadening their content knowledge. Classroom teachers, on the other hand, gain skills in working with students who learn in unique ways. The enhanced knowledge and skills of both partners benefit all the students these professionals serve, in and outside of the co-taught classroom.

> *The enhanced knowledge and skills of both partners benefit all the students these professionals serve, in and outside of the co-taught classroom.*

- Improved Instruction: Good instruction is served by connecting ideas. Innovation is usually the result of an idea that is germinated through a process of reflection, sharing, testing, and redesigning with collaborators. As Steven Johnson, author of *Where Good Ideas Come From*, writes "Good ideas want to connect, fuse, recombine. They want to reinvent themselves by crossing conceptual borders" (2010, 282). Research on professional learning communities, small groups of collaborative educators, shows the power of being able to tap into the collective creativity and wisdom of colleagues. Teachers who collaborate with colleagues develop instructional ideas that are more effective for students.

- Differentiation: Differentiated instruction is based on the premise that teachers should adapt instruction to meet students' varying readiness levels, learning preferences, and interests. Although most educators agree with this premise, they also agree that practical application is a challenge. Co-teaching makes differentiated instruction so much easier. Two heads and four hands make planning and implementing differentiation possible on a daily basis. Co-teachers bring different perspectives to lesson design, creating plans that include higher and lower levels of complexity and more hands-on applications. During instruction, partners flexibly group students as needed to ensure that all are learning at their highest levels. In addition, shared classroom management allows teachers to feel more comfortable with multiple learning activities taking place simultaneously in the room.

- Teacher Access: Students consistently report a preference for a co-taught classroom. Specifically, students comment, "If one teacher was busy, the other could help me" (Pittsford Central School District, 2006). Access to brief, individual assistance in the classroom allows students to get help immediately, rather than waiting for a tutorial or study hall later in the day. This means that students are able to continue learning with the class, rather than mentally dropping out due to poor comprehension and frustration.

- Behavior Management: One student made a complaint about his co-taught classroom, saying "When one's not watching you, the other is!" Behavior management is a natural outcome of a co-taught class because there are two sets of eyes for monitoring students, two bodies for proximity control, and two teachers to mix things up and make learning more interesting. When the occasional behavioral issue arises, one of the two teachers can intervene, removing the student if necessary, while the other can continue instruction for the rest of the class.

- Student Engagement: Several factors are related to high engagement. Robert Marzano and Debra Pickering, noted authors and researchers, identified the four major components of engagement as emotion, student interest, an understanding of importance, and a sense of efficacy (2010). A master teacher infuses one or more of these attributes in every lesson. But co-teachers can do this even more readily. Two adults can engage in a heated debate about a topic. Two adults can quickly generate connections to show the importance of the content to real life. Two adults can share multiple perspectives and multiple voices about a topic. Most importantly, two adults can easily create ways for students to do all of these things!

- Support for Unidentified Students: Many a teacher has lost sleep over the students who fall through the cracks—those students who are not identified for special services or extra help but are struggling. When specialists co-teach, they can use their expertise to have an impact on learning for all students in a class, not just those with labels. At a New York high school known for its high expectations, 86 percent of teachers surveyed felt that co-teaching gave them the opportunity to reach students who might otherwise be at risk of failure (Pittsford, 2006). Speech and occupational therapists, literacy specialists—so many educators who used to work with just identified students—embrace the opportunity to help all kids. Reading specialist Emily Kendig's enthusiasm is evident as she affirms, "It's about reaching the students who don't necessarily struggle enough to need pullout, but still need a little something extra" (personal communication, 2010).

- Time on Task: Pull-out models of service delivery in elementary schools usually involve students leaving their classroom in the midst of instruction to receive support in another space. If you have ever watched a young child walk through a school hallway, you know that the journey is not always quick or direct. Distractions abound, from peering into other classrooms and perusing the artwork hanging on the walls to chatting with friends and waving to teachers. All of this is lost instructional time—something struggling students cannot afford. Then, when they finally return to their classrooms, these students find that they have no idea what is going on. Instruction has proceeded without them. Teachers or peers have to try to catch them up to the rest—something struggling students do not do quickly. Co-teaching solves this problem.

> *Students' time on task is maximized because they do not leave the classroom.*

Students' time on task is maximized because they do not leave the classroom.

- Sense of Belonging: An inclusion advocate once linked the rising tide of teen suicide to the rising rates of students in special education. He voiced concern that students with disabilities, as well as other students, were receiving the message that people who were different didn't belong. Though this connection may seem a far stretch, we do know that students often admit feelings of embarrassment and isolation when they are removed from the classroom for services. The stigma associated with removal can leave a lasting impact. Co-teaching avoids these negative feelings by communicating the message that all students comprise the learning community, all students have strengths and weaknesses, and all students are worthwhile.

- Acceptance of Diversity: Take a look inside a truly inclusive classroom and you will see a kaleidoscope—students of different colors, sizes, talents—all blending together into one masterpiece of learning. Children who grow up in spaces where diversity is cherished are able to easily embrace diversity in the world around them. As global collaboration increases, graduates who are comfortable with diversity will be more successful.

- High Expectations: "I didn't know she could do that!" This exclamation is often heard when schools transition from pull-out services to inclusive education. Classroom teachers

> *Children who grow up in spaces where diversity is cherished are able to easily embrace diversity in the world around them.*

and specialists are frequently amazed by students who rise to the higher expectations of a general education setting. As far back as 1987, researchers were documenting that IEPs written for students in inclusive settings were of a higher quality on several dimensions considered to be best practices (Hunt, Goetz, and Anderson, 1986). This may be because a specialist working in isolation with atypical learners is likely to have a skewed sense of what students can do. Through co-teaching specialists broaden their sense of what students need to do, and more important, are capable of doing.

TO SUM UP

- Co-teaching is a coordinated instructional practice in which two or more educators simultaneously work with a heterogeneous group of students in a general education classroom.

- Research on co-teaching is limited, but professional educators report numerous benefits. The benefits that partners experience will depend on which co-teaching models they use and how effectively they work together.

DISCUSSION QUESTIONS

- Many definitions of co-teaching exist. What do you see as the key components of a definition that a school might choose to adopt?
- What does emerging research about co-teaching suggest?
- What benefits of co-teaching are teachers most likely to experience in the initial stages? In the later stages?

CHAPTER 2

Relationship Building

Common Challenges and Effective Solutions

Climate

In my workshops on inclusive schools, I frequently ask participants to complete the following simile:

The marriage between special education and general education is like . . .

After a few chuckles, participants silently begin to write their responses, some thinking of an answer immediately, while others stew for awhile. When it is time to share, the similes run the gamut from horror story to every teacher's dream.

The marriage between special education and general education is like . . . peanut butter and jelly—each good on their own but better together.

The marriage between special education and general education is like . . . being a one-legged man in a butt-kicking contest.

The marriage between special education and general education is like . . . an elderly couple—constantly bickering about trivial details but dependent on each other.

The marriage between special education and general education is like . . . a fine wine—it gets better with age.

The marriage between special education and general education is like . . . a divorced couple who try to communicate for the sake of their kids.

The marriage between special education and general education is like . . . a roller-coaster ride—sometimes thrilling, sometimes making you sick to your stomach.

The marriage between special education and general education is like . . . a hidden gem—just needs some elbow grease and polishing to make it shine.

Imagine doing this activity with your faculty. You provide them with blank index cards and ask them to complete the simile anonymously. When they are finished, you collect the cards and read the examples aloud. What would the overall tenor of the examples be? Mostly positive? Mostly negative? Somewhere in the middle? The vast majority of teachers believe that the similes would be heavily negative, reflective of their experiences.

These similes reveal a pervasive problem in our schools—a climate of separateness between specialists and classroom teachers. This climate originated in the 1960s and 1970s when districts began telling classroom teachers that only special education teachers had the skills necessary to teach students with disabilities. Federal legislation wasn't far behind. In 1973, special education was mandated through the passage of PL 94–142, the precursor to IDEA, the Individuals with Disabilities Education Act. *Special education* was defined in this legislation as "specially designed instruction to meet the unique needs of a child with a disability," and was meant to be seen as a service, not a place. But before long, self-contained programs proliferated, funding was separated, dual administrative structures were contrived, and we became mired in a climate of separateness.

After decades of "special," separate programs, beliefs about the best way to educate children with unique needs began to change. Pockets of success with inclusive classrooms led many educators to believe that collaborative services might be more effective than separate services. Individual voices like Marsha Forest, Richard Villa, and Marilyn Friend began to call for educators to cooperate, to bring their talents together to serve all children.

Unfortunately, attitude and climate do not always change quickly. There are some who say that change in education takes about thirty years—the time it takes for teachers to retire! However, change experts Chip and Dan Heath refute the notion that people (or teachers) inherently resist change. "In our lives we embrace lots of big changes—not only babies, but marriages and new homes and new technologies and new job duties. Meanwhile, other behaviors are maddeningly intractable" (2010, 4).

Do leaders need to accept dire predictions about the difficulty of changing attitudes and behaviors? Definitely not. Great leaders view dire circumstances as opportunities. Abraham Lincoln, in his Annual Message to Congress in 1862, pronounced: "The dogmas of the quiet past are inadequate to the stormy present. The occasion is piled high with difficulty and we must rise with the occasion. As our case is new, so we must think anew and act anew."

Proactive steps can be taken to develop a new climate of collaboration and inclusiveness. Dozens of ideas for promoting a healthy school climate have been suggested and implemented by leading educators (Mendez-Morse, 1992; Fullan, 2007; Hargreaves and Shirley, 2009; Freiberg, 1998; Chauncey, 2005; Sapon-Shevin, 2008). Specific steps for developing positive inclusive climates include:

- Creating a vision and mission statement that embraces collaborative relationships. Which comes first—the vision or the mission—is kind of like the argument about the chicken and the egg. What is not in dispute is the fact that organizations need a heart and a head—a belief and a set of processes and skills—to bring about change.

- Conducting a climate survey to identify subtle messages embedded in the physical environment (Beninghof and Singer, 1995). Research shows that our habits are woven into our environments. Small tweaks in an environment can make a difference.

- Ensuring that staff development programs integrate the needs of special populations into the content and discussion. Often, great ideas are presented in workshops but teachers are left to their own devices to figure out accommodations and adaptations at a later time. By building time for this into the original presentation, it ensures that all students will benefit.

- Providing adequate staff development on inclusion and co-teaching practices. The tone of the building can be greatly affected by the quantity and quality of professional development experiences. The best co-teaching occurs when all participants have a common knowledge base to build upon.

- Helping teachers to find common ground with colleagues. John Maxwell, leadership expert and author of *Everyone Communicates, Few Connect*, has found that connectors search for common ground—for common experiences to which both parties can relate (2010). When parties are aware of similar interests, they can use these to strengthen their relationships.

Potent, schoolwide efforts to build bridges between faculty members will lead to healthier relationships at the one-to-one level. Although it is not realistic to expect everyone on a faculty to agree on everything, it is realistic to expect collegial interactions for the sake of the students. Woodie Flowers, a professor emeritus at MIT, coined the term "gracious professionalism." Gracious professionalism refers to the blending of determination, respect, high quality work, and valuing of others. Teachers who embody the characteristics of gracious professionalism will be most successful at co-teaching.

> *Gracious professionalism refers to the blending of determination, respect, high quality work, and valuing of others. Teachers who embody the characteristics of gracious professionalism will be most successful at co-teaching.*

Climate is also important at the classroom level. Successful co-taught classrooms rely heavily on differentiated instruction, cooperative learning, and hands-on projects. The structures and strategies found in a co-taught classroom differ slightly from a typical class environment. Therefore, teaching partners will want to identify the climate attributes that they believe will most benefit their students. The following ingredients, when blended together, can create a nourishing learning environment.

- Individual differences are honored

  Mara Sapon-Shevin writes "Inclusion benefits all students by helping them understand and appreciate that the world is big, that people are different, and that we can work together to find solutions that work for everyone" (2008, 50).

- Fair treatment is not always equal treatment

  A common lament of children is "It's not fair!" Inclusion presents a wonderful opportunity to teach students the meaning of fairness. "In a strong co-teaching climate, both teachers clearly understand that fair means that everyone gets what he or she needs (and that fair does not mean that everyone gets the same or equal things). In inclusive classrooms where teachers are clear about fairness from the beginning and share their philosophy with students, this issue never arises" (Murawski and Dieker, 2008, 42).

- Mistakes are celebrated

    Creativity expert Sir Ken Robinson, in his popular TED Talk (2006) shared his concern about how kids deal with mistakes: "What we do know is, if you're not prepared to be wrong, you'll never come up with anything original. If you're not prepared to be wrong. And by the time they get to be adults, most kids have lost that capacity. They have become frightened of being wrong. And we run our companies like this, by the way. We stigmatize mistakes. And we're now running national education systems where mistakes are the worst thing you can make. And the result is that we are educating people out of their creative capacities."

    Teachers can turn this trend around by celebrating mistakes in the classroom. Imagine if every classroom welcomed students back to school with a "Celebrating Our Mistakes" bulletin board. From the first day of school, co-teachers can model that it is all right to make mistakes. They can also model the process of reflecting on mistakes to learn from them.

- Interactions are respectful

    Body language, tone of voice, words—all work together to convey a message. Students will watch teachers closely to pick up cues on how to interact with students that may seem different. If specialists use phrases such as "my kids can come to the station," students will begin to sense separateness. If students overhear adults using terms like "the ELLs" or "the Speds," especially if used with frustration in their tone, students will develop negative perspectives. Paula Denton, in her work with Responsive Classrooms, has seen the power of words over and over again. "By paying attention to our language, we can use it to open the doors of possibility for students" (2008, 30). Teachers who consistently model respectful interactions will find students following their lead.

- Contributions are expected

    Angela Maiers, educator and author, encourages teachers to swap out the word "share" with "contribute" when talking with students. A confident statement such as "We expect all students in this class to make contributions to our community" conveys a strong belief in the abilities of all, not just the students who are usually successful (2011).

- Interdependence is encouraged

The word "independence" is often included in school mission statements and goals. It makes sense that educators would want to develop independent thinkers and students who will be able to perform many tasks on their own. However, we know that "interdependence" is also a key characteristic of successful adults. Among other skills, students will need to negotiate shared responsibilities, flex their roles in group work, know when to seek out resources or help, and contribute their unique talents for the greater good.

Communication

Popular action films of recent years often include a rock climbing scene in which a couple of buff guys scale their way up the side of a cliff. Directors may show rock slippage, frayed ropes, or death-defying falls, but always the heroes emerge at the top after a few quick minutes and move on to their next challenge. Real rock climbing is not like this. In outdoor rock climbing, smart climbers communicate before beginning their route, while climbing each pitch, and after finishing the route. Before choosing a route, both climbers must be honest about their strengths and weaknesses. They must negotiate who will lead and who will follow, or if they will switch positions throughout the climb. Safe climbing partners review commands that will be used to communicate, especially in poor weather when voices may be swallowed up by winds. As they reach a ledge to rest, they check each other's equipment, energy levels, hydration, or injuries and make adjustments to their plan if necessary. When they finally reach the summit, celebration is in order—quickly followed by a debrief of how they handled the route and what they might do differently next time.

Bad communication between rock climbing partners is a recipe for disaster. Trevor Allred, climber and founder of Rockclimbing.com, describes the relationship: "You'll have to trust your climbing partner with your life. Beyond question. No mistakes allowed. This often makes for very strong bonds and relationships" (2010).

Co-teachers must also communicate effectively to accomplish their mission. While the results of poor communication may not be immediately life threatening, they can be life altering to the students in their classes. Teams that don't work well together are unlikely to produce high levels of learning. Leadership consultants Adrian Gostick and Chester Elton caution "No matter how talented the individuals on a team may be . . . if they are not communicating with one another openly and honestly they can get off course" (2010, 122).

Communication efforts begin as soon as two or more individuals are considering co-teaching together. Though it is common for teachers to feel that they know their colleagues, conversation about the following topics will help to fill in gaps and avoid assumptions.

> " *No matter how talented the individuals on a team may be . . . if they are not communicating with one another openly and honestly they can get off course.* "

- Teaching Philosophy: No need to write a formal philosophy statement or pull out your undergraduate paper. Informal but honest conversation about your beliefs will provide a sense of compatibility. How do you believe students learn best? What does good teaching look like? What is the ideal relationship between student and teacher? What word describes the role of the teacher—leader? facilitator? coach? giver? expert? boss?

- Teaching Goals: Obviously, all teachers will want their students to master the course content. Going beyond that, teachers should discuss other things they see as priorities. Do you want to foster critical thinking? Problem solving strategies? Twenty-first-century skills? Good citizenship? Cooperation? Stewardship of the planet? When team members have goals that are common or complementary, decisions about learning activities will be reached more readily.

- Personal and Professional Goals: Teaching partners may be at very different points in their lives. One may be raising a toddler while the other is approaching retirement. One might be attending graduate school for administrative licensure, while the other might be a new member of the PTA. Personal and professional goals will affect co-teaching. But they don't have to affect it negatively—if potential partners talk about them. Take a moment to reflect on your own personal and professional goals. What do you want to accomplish this year? What commitments have you made related to these goals? How might your goals affect your co-teaching? Once you and your colleague have articulated these, you can discuss any potential impact on your work together.

- Style: On the one hand, a benefit of co-teaching is that it brings together teachers with differing styles, strengths, and experiences—making instruction more applicable to a heterogeneous group of students. On the other hand, if teachers have drastically different styles, it may be difficult to work together effectively. The tortoise and the hare didn't end up as best buddies! Potential co-teaching partners should feel each other out for preferences about advanced planning, flexibility, time management, use of humor, classroom organization, noise tolerance, and level of assertiveness. The best co-teaching partners usually have styles that complement each other.

Once two teachers are engaged—they have committed to co-teach—they enter another level of communication. At this point, discussion needs to become much more focused on the nitty-gritty aspects of teaching a course and running a classroom. Avoid making assumptions about these aspects. Time constraints might cause teachers to feel that they can skip the talk and get right to the teaching. In the long run, this usually results in more time spent fixing problems arising out of assumptions. Various forms and checklists have been designed to make this process as efficient, yet thorough, as possible. Worksheet 2.1, the General Co-Teaching Practices Worksheet, covers a variety of topics that are inherent to the teaching process.

Partners will also benefit from discussing the various co-teaching models and deciding which ones to try. Exhibit 2.1, the Co-Teaching Models Checklist, will guide this discussion and assist in tracking decisions.

If co-teachers have front-loaded the process with effective communication, chances are they will be off and running smoothly. To keep running smoothly, they will need to grease the wheels with

WORKSHEET 2.1: General Co-Teaching Practices Worksheet

1. How will we introduce ourselves to our students? To parents?

2. How will we handle correspondence: parents, newsletters, e-mails, report cards?

3. Where will we keep confidential information regarding students?

4. What format will we use for lesson planning?

5. Will there be a designated space (desk, storage) in the room for Teacher B?

6. How will we arrange the room?

7. How will sub plans reflect our co-teaching relationship?

8. How will we handle disruptions (phone calls, visitor at the door, student behavior)?

9. How will we handle copying and other materials?

10. What classroom routines do we want to establish (restroom breaks, students late to class, missing assignments, attendance, pencil sharpening)?

11. What behavior management practices will we have in place? How will we respond to inappropriate behavior?

12. What will be our approach to homework?

13. What formative and summative assessment data will we collect? Where will we keep this information?

14. Which methods of communication will work best for us (e-mail, text, wikis, phone, face-to-face, online)?

15. When and where will we meet for co-planning and reflection?

16. What pet peeves do we each have?

EXHIBIT 2.1: Co-Teaching Models Checklist

Teachers: _____

MODEL	WE'LL TRY THIS ONE . . .	WE TRIED IT AND LIKED IT!	WE TRIED AND WILL PASS . . .
Duet			
Lead and Support			
Speak and Add			
Skill Groups			
Learning Style			
Station			
Parallel			
Adapting			
Complementary Skills			

continuous communication. During lesson planning meetings, partners will want to answer the following questions:

- How is it going? How well are students accomplishing the standards and objectives? What does assessment show?

- Where do we want to go next? What specific standards and objectives need to be taught?

- How will we differentiate? What methods or approaches can we utilize that will include various student learning styles, student interests, and readiness levels?

- What assessment procedures will be used to provide feedback?

- Which co-teaching models will work best? Which adult will take responsibilities for which tasks?

To the degree possible, partners should also try to take a few minutes each week to reflect on their co-teaching relationship. Grant Wiggins and Jay McTighe, in their powerful article "Examining the Teaching Life," advocate that "Learners attain understanding only through regular reflection, self-assessment and self-adjustment"(2006, 26–29). Co-teachers need to make time for vigorous questioning of their practices in order to determine what is and isn't working. On the practical side, some days it can be hard to find time to go the bathroom, much less sit down and vigorously question one's teaching practices. Formal reflection may not be possible as regularly as once per week, but should take place at least twice per semester. The Reflective Questions form (Exhibit 2.2) provides a structure for this dialogue.

In the mid-1960s, a psychologist named Bruce Tuckman suggested that all teams go through four stages of development. Borrowing from the field of poetry, Tuckman named these stages Forming, Storming, Norming, and Performing. His theory has been applied to many different fields and applies well to the development of co-teaching teams. In particular, Tuckman claimed that the second stage, Storming, was essential to the health of any team that wanted to perform well over the long haul. Storming, the process of open, honest discussion about differences, doesn't have to be as volatile as the name suggests, but it does have to occur. Because no two teachers are a matched pair of shoes, differences will arise as they work together day after day. Some of these differences will be inconsequential, while others may have a grave impact on student learning. These need to be discussed.

EXHIBIT 2.2: Reflective Questions for Co-Teaching Teams

Where does our team fall on the continuum below, in each of the various areas?

◄───►

Minimal Effectiveness   Maximum Effectiveness

AREA	GUIDING QUESTIONS/THOUGHTS/EXAMPLES
Level of Engagement: Students	How engaged are the students? What else can we do to keep them more engaged? • Vocal qualities • Role switching • Debating • Group work • Paper tasks
Level of Engagement: Adults	Are there times when one adult is underutilized? Are all adults feeling fully utilized? Are there talents that we are not using? When one is leading, what are things the other adult(s) can be doing? How comfortable and confident are we with our roles?
Differentiation	How are we adapting? Are we addressing IEP objectives? Are we addressing the needs of students who are ready for more? Are we teaching the necessary "access skills" as well as curricular content? Do we have the planning time to accomplish differentiation? Is our planning time structured to facilitate our goals?
Environment	Does the physical layout of the room support co-teaching? Are we using technology in an interactive manner? Are there ways that one or both adults could use technology in the class that may not be possible in a solo taught class? Do our handouts/tests, etc., incorporate adaptations such as font choice and type size? What message does the classroom send about the roles of the adults—i.e., is it **Mr. Jones' Class** or **Mr. Jones' and Ms. Smith's Class**? Do we have duplicate sets of books, amplification devices, etc.? Do we use "our" language vs. "my" language?

Many teachers are reluctant to enter into difficult conversations. At my workshops, it is common for a co-teacher to share with me her frustration about her partnership. When I ask whether she has talked honestly with her partner about it, the response is usually "no." Susan Scott, communication expert, suggests that success at work and in life comes about through authentic conversations. "While many fear 'real' it is the unreal conversation that should scare us to death. Unreal conversations are expensive . . . no one has to change. When the conversation is real, the change occurs before the conversation is over" (2004, xv). If teachers approach the "storming" with authenticity, respect, and flexibility, positive outcomes will occur for teachers and students.

A teacher can increase the likelihood of positive outcomes by keeping the following points in mind during difficult co-teaching discussions:

- Figure out your own communication and thinking style. Compare it to your partner's, and then try to match his or her style as much as possible when trying to convey an important point. Effective communicators have one of the positive attributes of a chameleon—they can adapt to fit their surroundings.

- If you don't understand your partner's point of view, ask for help. Phrases such as "Help me understand your point of view" or "What do you need?" communicate to your partner that you are truly interested. Effective problem solvers ask many questions for each statement they offer. A ratio of 10:1 leads to a wealth of information to inform the decision making process.

- Validate by rephrasing your partner's comments. Authentic validation decreases defensive reactions. But be sure to be authentic. Nothing can be as irritating in a difficult discussion as someone offering a patronizing "What I hear you saying is . . . " Authentic rephrasing also ensures accurate understanding. Chip and Dan Heath, experts on bringing about change, claim "What looks like resistance is often a lack of clarity" (2010, 17).

- Be flexible with your personal time line. Perhaps the conversation will need to take place over a few days. Providing time for each person to reflect and reconsider is much healthier for a relationship over the long run than pushing too hard for a quick resolution.

- Be present. Choose a time and a place for the conversation where you can devote your entire attention—your presence—to the exchange. The power of presence is immensely affirming to the relationship. It says "I feel this time together is important and valuable, and I am fully committed to it." Presence will yield positive outcomes that last well beyond the difficult conversation.

Roles and Responsibilities

Picture the last holiday meal shared by your extended family. Mom (usually) is in charge in the kitchen. Bustling about, she is trying to manage the preparation of multiple dishes, stay on top of the ever-growing pile of dirty pots and pans, and strategically plan it all to arrive on the table at the scheduled time. A secret observer may overhear a few muttered curses, some "Yum, that's good," and even a strident "I could use some help in here!" The well-meaning spouse or children quickly arrive and offer their assistance. Everybody jumps in, reaching over each other, bumping elbows, offering their cooking advice, and chatting pleasantly.

Many of us can relate to this picture. But just as many can probably picture times when Mom preferred to go it alone. An old proverb captures it well—"Too many cooks spoil the broth." As more hands participate in the completion of a task, the roles and responsibilities can become blurred. Whose job is it to be the head cook? Who has to scrub the pots and pans? Who gets to add the spice? Who cleans up the mess?

As more hands participate in the completion of a task, the roles and responsibilities can become blurred.

A similar confusion can occur in a co-taught classroom. Two teachers, often with years of solo experience, must find a way to share or divide responsibilities to achieve the best student outcomes. This process is complicated by a number of factors:

- Ego
- Areas of expertise
- Philosophy of education
- Values

- Past experiences
- Personal and professional goals
- Personality traits
- Cognitive styles
- Sense of time

Explicit communication about roles and responsibilities is essential to success. Partners who fail to engage in this discussion often report frustration over a lack of parity (Dieker and Murawski, 2003). One partner may assume that the other partner has the same vision for the division of responsibilities. Take the following example:

> Mrs. Martin and Mrs. Colfax had taught in the same building for more than ten years. Often they chatted over lunch, swapped teaching ideas, and helped each other with decorating bulletin boards. So when their principal asked them to co-teach together, they readily accepted, looking forward to using the power of their friendship to benefit their students. Unfortunately, the school did not provide any staff development on co-teaching, so the two teachers were left to figure it out on their own. Many hours were spent over the summer planning units, arranging the furniture and discussing strategies. Three weeks into the school year, after several days of unruly student behavior, Mrs. Martin experienced an "aha" moment in the middle of class. It dawned on her that Mrs. Colfax had been managing the behavior of the general education students only, leaving the behavioral issues of the special education students solely to Mrs. Martin. Both teachers had made assumptions about the other's behavior management philosophies and how best to handle this responsibility in the classroom. They had never discussed this topic, assuming—because they knew each other well—that they would have similar beliefs.

The word for this problem is "assumicide." According to www.urbandictionary.com, "when your assumptions lead to dire consequences that could lead to your potential demise, you commit assumicide." Too many co-teaching relationships fail simply because teachers have never talked about how best to share roles and responsibilities. Although some guidance can be mined from federal and state law, responsibility for many of the day-to-day tasks is left to each unique partnership to determine.

The Co-Teaching Responsibility Checklist (Exhibit 2.3) offers partners a structure for discussing the many responsibilities that arise throughout the instructional cycle (Beninghof and Singer, 1995). Etta Hollins, in her research with urban schools, found that "Structured dialogue is a powerful instrument for empowering teachers" (2006). Decisions reached by using this structured checklist are not lodged in cement, but can be reexamined as the year progresses. In addition, teams can add their own list of crucial tasks and responsibilities by completing the Additional Tasks Checklist (Exhibit 2.4), and adding to it as new issues arise. Tasks on this checklist may include mundane things such as:

- Making copies
- Decorating bulletin boards
- Arranging field trips
- Scheduling parent conferences
- Supervising detentions
- Planning holiday parties
- Stapling and cutting
- Filing papers
- Taking attendance
- Fulfilling recess, hall, or bus duty obligations
- Writing the daily schedule, agenda, or objectives on the board
- Cleaning up the classroom
- Tracking missing assignments
- Posting to the class blog
- Managing materials distribution and collection
- Contacting the janitor, IT department, nurse, or counselor
- Ordering supplies

As co-teachers discuss their roles and responsibilities, a heightened sense of clarity will emerge. This clarity can provide

EXHIBIT 2.3: Collaborative Teaching Responsibilities Checklist

WHO WILL BE RESPONSIBLE FOR:	NAME	NAME	SHARED	COMMENTS
Identifying goals and objectives for the course?				
Designing individualized objectives for the targeted students?				
Planning instructional activities to achieve the goals?				
Selecting and organizing instructional materials?				
Teaching specific class content?				
Teaching study skills and learning strategies?				
Collecting data on student performance?				
Establishing and implementing grading procedures?				
Establishing and implementing a classroom management plan?				
Maintaining home contact?				
Modifying curriculum and materials as necessary?				
Designing tests, homework assignments, etc.?				
Providing individual assistance to students?				
Taking care of daily routines (for example attendance, lunch counts)?				
Directing paraeducators, parent volunteers, and/or other support personnel?				
Communicating to all appropriate parties regarding the targeted students?				

EXHIBIT 2.4: Additional Tasks Checklist

Directions: List the various tasks and responsibilities that are essential for your team to function well and achieve your goals. Discuss the tasks with your partner(s) and reach a conclusion in each case regarding who will bear the responsibility for the tasks.

WHO WILL BE RESPONSIBLE FOR:	NAME	NAME	NAME	SHARED

renewed teaching vigor, as each individual realizes that she is not alone. In *The Well-Balanced Teacher*, Mike Anderson writes:

> There's no doubt that teaching is a tough profession, and it doesn't seem to be getting any easier. Teachers manage an incredible array of roles and responsibilities including planning and teaching lessons, communicating with parents, collaborating with colleagues, and staying current on educational trends and new legal policies. From No Child Left Behind to peanut-free cafeteria tables to professional learning communities to arts and technology in the classroom, teachers have a lot of responsibilities to juggle. Whether good or bad, these new trends seem to be accelerating at an alarming rate and show no signs of slowing down. (2010)

Healthy, balanced collegial sharing can extend the life of the co-teaching relationship. Instead of attempting to control and manage all these responsibilities as a solo teacher, co-teachers can lighten their load and their spirits.

TO SUM UP

- School and classroom climate will have a large impact on the success of co-teaching. Teachers and administrators can take simple steps to ensure that everyone feels included and valued.

- Clear, honest communication between partners is essential. Communication can be guided through the use of a variety of tools and checklists.

- Partners should delineate their roles and responsibilities before they begin co-teaching so that the strengths of both adults are fully utilized.

DISCUSSION QUESTIONS

- Describe the current climate of your school as it relates to inclusive education. What are its strengths and weaknesses?
- How will your personal strengths help you to address any of the co-teaching challenges?
- What steps might be taken to encourage reluctant or resistant co-teachers?

CHAPTER 3

Implementation

Common Challenges
and Effective Solutions

Classroom Composition

Early inclusion advocates argued in favor of the principle of natural proportions when composing class rosters. This principle suggests that inclusive education will be most effective if the classroom makeup mirrors the makeup of the community at large. In other words, if the community is composed of 15 percent persons with disabilities, then the classroom should not have more than 15 percent students with disabilities. Generally, this results in spreading targeted students across all classes at any grade level so that there is a natural, heterogeneous classroom community.

The principle of natural proportions results in some significant benefits and one significant challenge. Classrooms composed with this principle in mind include lots of appropriate role models, allow all students in a school the opportunity to befriend targeted students, and ensure that no single teacher will be overwhelmed with increased responsibilities. But because targeted students are spread across many classrooms, the specialists who serve them must also be spread across many classrooms, making it almost impossible to co-teach. It is the rare school that has sufficient staffing to make effective co-teaching a reality in every class.

Cluster grouping is the next best thing. Cluster grouping refers to the process of assigning a higher than natural proportion of targeted students to a class for the purpose of efficient and effective service delivery. For example, a second grade at Summit School may have three classrooms with seventy-five students, eight of whom have been identified as needing special education. If the eight students are spread across all three classes, the special education teacher will need to schedule time in all three rooms and plan with all three teachers, in addition to her caseload at other grade levels. Clustering those eight students into two of the rooms, or even into one room, will reduce the scheduling challenge and allow the specialist to be more focused.

Caution must be taken when clustering targeted students. A classroom can quickly become a dumping ground for all the struggling students in a grade. The thinking might be "They have two teachers in there so they can handle it." Practitioners all agree—once the percentage of targeted students in a co-taught class passes 30 percent, benefits can deteriorate. For cluster grouping to be effective, the remainder of the class should be composed of on-grade level and above-grade level students, with a natural variety of demographic characteristics.

Cluster grouping has its drawbacks. Unless the specialist will be in the classroom all day, there will be chunks of time when the general education teacher will have to teach and manage the targeted students on her own. It may be difficult to find a general education teacher willing to take on this greater responsibility. Creative administrators may consider offering perks, such as smaller class size or reduced duties, as an enticement.

> *Practitioners all agree—once the percentage of targeted students in a co-taught class passes 30 percent, benefits can deteriorate.*

Planning Time

> *Mastering time is no task for the faint of heart.*
>
> —R. Alec Mackenzie

Finding adequate time to co-plan is considered by teachers to be the biggest challenge, and the biggest solution, to co-teaching. Fundamental to crafting top-notch instructional programs is time for partners to think, talk, plan, create, and reflect. Steven Johnson, best-selling author and innovation expert, describes the development of good ideas in his book *Where Good Ideas Come From*. "Most great ideas first take shape in a partial, incomplete form. They have the seeds of something profound, but they lack a key element that can turn the hunch into something truly powerful. And more often than not, that missing element is somewhere else, living as another hunch in another person's head" (2010, 851).

Johnson calls this process "the slow hunch." Rather than the eureka moments that are immortalized in stories or film, most good ideas take time to develop through collaborative interaction with others. If schools genuinely want to improve the quality of learning for students, educators must have time for collegial collaboration.

> "*Fundamental to crafting top-notch instructional programs is time for partners to think, talk, plan, create, and reflect.*"

How do we find the time? Schools all over the country are grappling with this question. Some of the solutions they find are small, short-term fixes, while others are more systemic, addressing the problem on a long-term basis. There is a single thread that runs throughout every success story—administrative support. School administrators who view co-planning time as a top, sacrosanct priority manage to make it happen.

One popular and effective strategy is often referred to as the "Roaming Sub Strategy." Once a month, a sign-up sheet is placed in the office, divided into two columns, with thirty or forty-five minute time blocks down the left-hand side. General education teachers write their name in one of the blocks in the left-hand column, and the name of their specialist in opposite block. One or two substitutes are brought in to cover for the teachers, roaming in short time blocks from class to class throughout the day.

Administrators have also found another way to utilize substitutes— without additional expenses. When a substitute covers for a teacher, there is usually a period (or two) during the day designated as a "prep." Because substitutes don't do "prep," their time is usually spent waiting for the minute hand to move along. Some creative principals have recognized this wasted resource and are putting substitutes to work during the prep period by having them support or cover for a co-teacher. Office staff can be enlisted to make these arrangements in the morning as soon as a teacher has called in sick.

Many schools have a day each week where they hold several meetings in a row to develop Individualized Education Plans for students in special education. Typically, a substitute is brought in so that general education teachers can attend the meetings. If these meetings do not fill the entire day, the substitute can cover a co-teacher's class so that she has an additional planning opportunity. In addition, when substitutes are brought in for a half day of meetings, some schools just hire the person for the entire day. The difference in cost is usually minimal, yet can yield several extra hours of coverage for collaboration activities.

Low-maintenance academic activities can also provide opportunities for extra planning time with no additional cost. One school found that sustained silent reading (SSR) was just such an activity. Sustained silent reading has been found to have positive effects on reading achievement (Garan and DeVoogd, 2008) As an added bonus, SSR requires very little teacher direction. Because of this, teachers are able to double up classes for SSR, freeing one teacher for additional collaboration time. Other schools have had similar success with study halls, assemblies, community service, guest lecturers, and student leadership meetings.

Another no-cost strategy is to have administrators and other specialists teach one class every few weeks. Many teachers roll their eyes at this strategy; however, most professionals who currently hold roles outside the classroom love the idea of teaching once in a while. By considering all the people in a building who may be able to step into a teaching role once in a while, the effect can add up. For example, in one building you may be able to utilize the principal, assistant principal, counselor, special education supervisor, curriculum specialist, school psychologist, and reading specialist. This would provide seven extra blocks of coverage—perhaps enough to offer each of your co-teaching general educators one extra planning period. In addition, the renewed empathy for classroom teachers that the administrators experience leads to stronger relationships within the building.

Flexible schedules, or "flex time," can bring a simple solution to collaboration between a classroom teacher and a paraeducator. Paraeducators usually support several classrooms and are assigned to be with students from the first to last bell of the school day. Because this eliminates their availability during prep periods, co-teachers end up in a catch-as-catch-can mode for planning with paraeducators. One school used flex time to solve this problem. Paraeducators were allowed to leave a half hour early one day during the week in exchange for staying a half hour late another day of the week. This allowed the paraeducators to meet with their co-teachers after school to discuss instructional issues.

Inclusion advocate Richard Villa suggests using "serendipitous times" for planning (Villa, Thousand, and Nevin, 2004.) For example, if school is delayed or closed due to snow, teachers could spend an additional hour co-planning. This has become an even better idea since the advent of web tools, such as Skype, which allow teachers to talk face-to-face over the Internet. Cloud-based collaborative writing tools, wikis, and social communication tools expand co-planning opportunities beyond the traditional school day parameters. One elementary co-teaching team accomplishes most of its co-planning through the use of a grade-level wiki—uploading and revising lesson plans, assessments, slide shows—only touching base during the class period and over the occasional lunch.

Meaty discussion at staff meetings may result in creative ideas for finding collaborative time. Teachers are the ones most affected by a lack of planning time and will be the most motivated to solve it. Daniel Pink, in his paradigm-shattering book on motivation entitled *Drive*, dispels old theories of motivation as not fitting within today's flat, globally connected world. He reiterates what the research concludes: "Human beings have an innate drive to be autonomous, self-determined and connected to one another. When that drive is liberated, people achieve more and live richer lives" (2009, 71). School leaders who recognize this power can liberate teachers to create collaborative planning solutions.

For longer-range solutions, schools may also want to explore one or more of the following ideas:

- Lengthening the school day four days per week, with an early dismissal for students on the fifth day. After students leave, teachers can spend time collaborating with colleagues.

- Repurposing staff development days to allow some of the time to be used for team planning.

- Lengthening the school year for teachers so that a few extra days are available before school begins and during the year to plan with colleagues.

- Using blended learning (a combination of in-school and online instruction) to decrease real-time contact with students, thus increasing time for collaboration.

- Hiring a long-term substitute to work with several schools, rotating among them to provide necessary coverage.

- Obtaining grants to pay stipends to teachers for extensive planning meetings beyond the contracted school day or year.

Grading

There is a fairly common workshop activity used by staff developers to open a discussion about grading. Each participant is given the same copy of a student's spelling test and asked to grade it privately, giving the student a number and letter grade. No questions are allowed. Teachers then share the grades they gave the student. Inevitably, the grades range from Ds to As. How can this happen with something as objective as spelling? The answer is that grading is a very complicated, subjective, values-laden process. It is difficult enough when one teacher is grading by himself, but can become even more challenging when grading is shared with a colleague.

Many school districts have attempted to lessen the complexity of grading by developing clear policies and procedures to follow. If these are in place, co-teachers should follow them. If the district or school does not have specific guidelines, then co-teachers will find it helpful to discuss the questions included in Exhibit 3.1, Co-Teaching Grading Questions. In most cases, there are not "right" or "wrong" answers—just different opinions. Partners should attempt to reach consensus before presenting their grading policy to their students.

> *Partners should attempt to reach consensus before presenting their grading policy to their students.*

When co-teachers have students with disabilities in their class, the IEP or 504 plan must be reviewed carefully for any agreements related to grading. Because these documents are legal agreements, teachers must follow them. Sometimes grading-related items are very obvious, such as statements about reduced workload or modified curriculum. Other times there may be grading-related items that are more subtle, such as "extended time." It is the responsibility of both teachers to be familiar with the contents of these plans and follow the decisions found in them.

EXHIBIT 3.1: Co-Teaching Grading Questions

- In general, how do you grade students?
- Should we take a student's effort, participation, punctuality, or attendance into account?
- Should we ever grade on a curve? Under what circumstances?
- Should a student's individual progress be taken into account in the grade?
- Should we ever give the benefit of the doubt? If so, when?
- How often should we use a rubric for assignments and grading?
- What is your feeling about extra time to complete assignments?
- Should we allow partial credit for late work?
- What are your beliefs or practices about extra credit?
- Will students get a 0 for missing work?
- Does neatness count in grading?
- Is it ever OK to fail a student?
- How do you feel about varied options for showing learning?
- If a student does less complex work, can he still achieve an A? If a student does more difficult work, does that automatically mean he receives an A?
- How do you feel about grading students as a group? Should they be graded on group skills, content mastery, or both?
- Which accommodations are you comfortable with during test taking? Which cause you concern?
- Should more recent scores in a semester carry greater weight than earlier ones?
- How do you feel about students ever grading their own work? Grading peer's work?
- Should we differentiate grades based on process, product, and soft skills?
- How will we communicate "OUR" grading policy to students? To parents?

Evaluation

The pressure is on for education to become more and more data-based. At the end of the day, we want to be able to answer the question: "Is it working?" As mentioned in Chapter One, there is a paucity of research on the effectiveness of co-teaching, perhaps because there are so many variables that make it difficult to define. However there are still simple ways that schools can evaluate their efforts.

Student feedback can be eye-opening. One school district disseminated a student survey near the end of their first year of co-teaching in middle school. After several questions with a Likert scale response, the survey allowed students space to write a comment. Almost a third of the students wrote in "I liked having a helper in the classroom" (or its equivalent). Though positive in nature, this comment conveys a worrisome underutilization of the second teacher in the class; a picture of one teacher in charge while the other operates as a second-class citizen. Receiving this feedback from students was much more powerful than a year of administrator comments about parity.

Another school, using a similar student survey, found that some students commented about feeling that the curriculum had been dumbed down in the co-taught class. This feedback immediately raised some tough discussions about insuring rigor while also providing adaptations. Again, students' perspectives are powerful.

The following Student Survey (Worksheet 3.1) can be reproduced and adapted to fit the specific information a school wants to gather from its students.

Parent reactions to co-teaching are also an important piece of program evaluation. Many school reform efforts emphasize that parents are paramount to success. One of the ways to increase parent involvement, and thereby increase student achievement, is to ask for their feedback about their child's educational experience. The Parent Survey (Worksheet 3.2) can be reproduced for this purpose.

Teachers are also stakeholders in any co-teaching initiative and should have the opportunity to share their reactions. Focus groups and staff meetings can be organized for teachers to voice their experiences, ideas, and concerns. Open dialogue about what's working and what's not can engage everyone in the problem-solving process. However,

WORKSHEET 3.1: Student Survey

Directions: We want to know how you felt about your co-taught class. Circle the number that best describes your opinion for each item.

1 = strongly disagree

2 = disagree

3 = neutral

4 = agree

5 = strongly agree

1. I enjoyed having two teachers in this class.	1	2	3	4	5
2. I received more help in this class than in classes taught by just one teacher.	1	2	3	4	5
3. All students were treated as equals.	1	2	3	4	5
4. I liked the variety of activities in this class.	1	2	3	4	5
5. I think I learn more when I have two teachers.	1	2	3	4	5
6. The class is more well behaved when we have two teachers.	1	2	3	4	5
7. I would like to have two teachers in my other classes.	1	2	3	4	5

Do you have anything else you want to say about your co-taught class?

_____

_____

_____

WORKSHEET 3.2: Parent Survey

Directions: We would like your feedback on the co-taught class(es) in which your child has participated. Please take a moment to circle the number that best describes your opinion, and return the survey in the envelope provided.

1 = strongly disagree

2 = disagree

3 = neutral

4 = agree

5 = strongly agree

1. My child enjoyed having two teachers in class.	1	2	3	4	5
2. My child received more assistance by having two teachers in class.	1	2	3	4	5
3. My child benefited from being in a co-taught class.	1	2	3	4	5
4. I would like my child to have more co-taught classes.	1	2	3	4	5
5. I was adequately informed about the co-teaching program.	1	2	3	4	5
6. Communication with the teachers in the co-taught class was sufficient.	1	2	3	4	5
7. My child does better in a co-taught class.	1	2	3	4	5

Do you have anything else you want to say about your child's experience in a co-taught class?

_____

_____

_____

some teachers may be more vocal than others, skewing the data gathered. Private or anonymous surveys may result in additional data that can be used for program improvement. The following Teacher Survey (Worksheet 3.3) has been used with success by a variety of school districts, and can be reproduced and adapted to fit your needs.

Self-reporting surveys provide one type of information for schools to explore. But more objective information can sometimes be gathered by observation. Observations can be formal or informal, with a variety of evaluative purposes. The Co-Teaching Observation Tool (Worksheet 3.4) was designed for informal observations, to give both administrators and teachers an idea of what an effective co-taught classroom might look like. With an area for open-ended evidence, it recognizes that co-teaching must look different from class to class and from time to time if teachers are truly addressing the diverse needs of their students.

> *Open dialogue about what's working and what's not can engage everyone in the problem-solving process.*

Student engagement rates can be a powerful type of data for evaluating the benefits of co-teaching versus solo teaching. Student engagement has been correlated with increased academic achievement and decreased dropout rates, both of which are compatible with the goals of co-teaching. Teachers know that when students are fully engaged they are more likely to be learning than when they are off task, distracted, or underinvolved. Common sense would suggest that engagement rates would be higher in an effective co-taught class. But engagement is a complex concept, including multiple dimensions. In 2004, researchers Fredericks, Blumenthal, and Paris proposed that engagement can be viewed as a combination of behavioral, emotional, and cognitive factors. For each of these factors, different measurement tools might be needed. In 2011, the National Center for Education Evaluation and Regional Assistance published a review of twenty-one tools that can be used for measuring student engagement (Fredricks et al., 2011). This document describes, in detail, the purposes of each tool and its psychometric properties.

The Instructional Practices Inventory (Table 3.1), originally developed by Painter and Valentine (1996), is a practical tool for profiling student engagement for the purpose of schoolwide conversations about engagement. Although not initially designed for

WORKSHEET 3.3: Teacher Survey

Directions: We would like your feedback on the co-taught class(es) in which you have been involved. Please take a moment to circle the number that best describes your opinion, and return the survey in the envelope provided.

General education teacher _____

Specialist _____

1 = strongly disagree

2 = disagree

3 = neutral

4 = agree

5 = strongly agree

1. Co-teaching is an initiative that should continue.	1	2	3	4	5
2. Targeted students learn better in co-taught classes than they did previously.	1	2	3	4	5
3. Students' behavior is better in co-taught classes than in traditional classes.	1	2	3	4	5
4. Co-teaching is benefiting average students.	1	2	3	4	5
5. Students in co-taught classes show greater acceptance of diverse abilities than students in traditional classes.	1	2	3	4	5
6. Teachers who co-teach experience professional growth and improve their teaching skills.	1	2	3	4	5

Additional comments:

_____

_____

_____

WORKSHEET 3.4: Co-Teaching Observation Tool

Teachers:_____ **Date:**_____

Roles	Evidence
Both teachers are actively engaged in the teaching/learning process for 95% of the lesson.	
The specialist integrates his or her unique teaching expertise into the lesson.	
Professionalism	**Evidence**
Students view both adults as "teachers" with equal authority.	
Interactions between teachers show respect for each other.	
Teachers feel equally responsible for what happens in the classroom.	
Communication	**Evidence**
Teachers share responsibility for major decisions regarding the instructional cycle.	
Teachers have time to plan lessons together and discuss issues related to instruction.	
Assessment	**Evidence**
Assessments are modified as necessary.	
Progress on IEP objectives is monitored frequently.	
Both teachers are aware of IEP objectives.	
Learning behaviors are being frequently monitored.	
Grading is a shared task.	
Instruction	**Evidence**
Various grouping arrangements are used to facilitate learning.	
Instructional strategies are utilized that enhance the learning of struggling students.	
The instructional lead is shared, depending on the needs of the students.	
Students with IEPs are included so that their participation is as normal as possible.	
Student work is differentiated, if necessary, to meet the needs of students.	

Additional Comments:

_____

_____

_____

Table 3.1 Instructional Practices Inventory Categories

		Student Engagement in Higher-Order Deeper Learning
Student Active Engaged Learning (6)	Students are engaged in higher-order thinking and developing deeper understanding through analysis, problem solving, critical thinking, creativity, and/or synthesis. Engagement in learning is not driven by verbal interaction with peers, even in a group setting. Examples of classroom practices commonly associated with higher-order/deeper Active Engaged Learning include: inquiry-based approaches such as project-based and problem-based learning; research and discovery/exploratory learning; authentic demonstrations; independent metacognition, reflective journaling, and self-assessment; and higher-order responses to higher-order questions.	
Student Verbal Learning Conversations (5)	Students are engaged in higher-order thinking and developing deeper understanding through analysis, problem solving, critical thinking, creativity, and/or synthesis. The higher-order/deeper thinking is driven by peer verbal interaction. Examples of classroom practices commonly associated with higher-order/deeper Verbal Learning Conversations include: collaborative or cooperative learning; peer tutoring, debate, and questioning; partner research and discovery/exploratory learning; Socratic learning; and small group or whole class analysis and problem solving, metacognition, reflective journaling, and self-assessment. Conversations may be teacher stimulated but are not teacher dominated.	

TABLE 3.1 Instructional Practices Inventory Categories—cont'd

Teacher-Led Instruction (4)	Students are attentive to teacher-led instruction as the teacher leads the learning experience by disseminating the appropriate content knowledge and/or directions for learning. The teacher provides basic content explanations, tells or explains new information or skills, and verbally directs the learning. Examples of classroom practices commonly associated with Teacher-Led Instruction include: teacher dominated question/answer; teacher lecture or verbal explanations; teacher direction giving; and teacher demonstrations. Discussions may occur, but instruction and ideas come primarily from the teacher. Student higher order/deeper learning is not evident.	**Student Engagement in Knowledge and Skill Development**
Student Work with Teacher Engaged (3)	Students are engaged in independent or group work designed to build basic understanding, new knowledge, and/or pertinent skills. Examples of classroom practices commonly associated with Student Work with Teacher Engaged include: basic fact finding; building skill or understanding through practice, "seatwork," worksheets, chapter review questions; and multi-media with teacher viewing media with students. The teacher is attentive to, engaged with, or supportive of the students. Student higher-order/deeper learning is not evident.	
Student Work with Teacher not Engaged (2)	This category is the same as Category 3 except the teacher is not attentive to, engaged with, or supportive of the students. The teacher may be out of the room, working at the computer, grading papers, or in some form engaged in work not directly associated with the students' learning. Student higher-order/deeper learning is not evident.	
Student Disengagement (1)	Students are not engaged in learning directly related to the curriculum.	**Students Not Engaged**

The Instructional Practices Inventory categories were developed by Bryan Painter and Jerry Valentine in 1996. Valentine refined the descriptions of the categories (2002, 2005, 2007, and 2010). The IPI was developed to profile schoolwide student engaged learning and was not designed for, nor should it be used for, personnel evaluation. For information about the IPI Process, contact Jerry Valentine at ValentineJ@Missouri.edu.

Reprinted herein by permission from the author, August 2011. Copying permitted only by written permission of author at ValentineJ@Missouri.edu.

co-teaching evaluation, Valentine contends that the process can have value in providing insights into the benefits of co-teaching. Observers, after undergoing the required one-day training, have demonstrated .80–.90 interrater reliability. Coupled with documented validity, the Instructional Practices Inventory can provide schools with research-based evidence of success.

TO SUM UP

- Cluster grouping, placing a slightly larger-than-normal number of target students in a room, may be necessary in order to staff for co-teaching. Although educators should take some precautions with cluster grouping, it can be used very effectively.

- Co-teaching partners must have common planning time in order to be effective. Schools have found myriad ways to build this into busy schedules.

- Educators bring different perspectives and values to the grading process. Co-grading will require partners to review IEPs, discuss grading philosophies, and reach consensus about grading practices.

- To ensure that the co-teaching program is continually improving, evaluative efforts should include students, teachers, parents, and administrators.

DISCUSSION QUESTIONS

- What precautions should teachers take when their classroom composition goes beyond natural proportions?

- Discuss various co-planning time options. Which might be the most effective?

- Numerous questions about grading beliefs and practices have been presented. If you had to choose only five questions to discuss with a co-teacher, which would they be? Why?

- Why is it important to ask parents and students for their feedback on co-teaching?

PART TWO

LOOKING THROUGH THE CO-TEACHING KALEIDOSCOPE

Models of Co-Teaching

Co-teaching is most successful when each partnership is encouraged to develop a model that works best for their students. Within the course of a single week, within the course of a single lesson, the teachers might move in and out of several different models or approaches to co-teaching. This book will present nine models of co-teaching from which to pick and choose (see Table P2.1 for an overview). The number of models presented by any text or consultant is somewhat arbitrary given that there are really unlimited ways that two teachers can work together.

Because co-teachers may come from many different fields of education, such as speech and language, literacy, or ELL, each model will be described in terms of the roles of Teacher A and Teacher B. The term "specialist" will be used to refer to the adult that is not the general educator. The phrase "targeted students" will be used to refer to students who are the focus of the specialist's intervention, such as students identified as gifted or in need of special education. In subsequent chapters, the unique factors of co-teaching in each specialty area will be explored in further depth. In addition to role descriptions, the pros and cons of each model will be outlined to assist in your selection of a model that is best suited to the circumstances.

TABLE P2.1: A Synopsis of Co-Teaching Models

	DESCRIPTION	PROS	CONS
Duet	Both teachers share the entire instructional process.	Most integrated for students Fully utilizes all expertise	Most time intensive
Lead and Support	Teacher A does advanced planning in isolation. Teacher B is fully involved in daily planning, implementation, and assessment.	Both teachers involved in most phases of instruction Saves time for Teacher B	Less input in planning for differentiation
Speak and Add	Teacher A leads and Teacher B adds visually or verbally.	Little co-planning time Almost anyone can do this	Can step on toes Underutilization of Teacher B's expertise
Skill Groups	Teachers divide students into more homogeneous ability groups and provide leveled instruction.	Multiple readiness levels are addressed Focused expertise	Possible feel of "tracking"
Station	Teacher A leads the class while Teacher B pulls a small group of students to the side of the room for direct instruction.	Intense, direct instruction for a small group of students	May be embarrassing for students who are pulled aside
Learning Style	Teachers plan lesson and divide responsibilities by learning modalities. Teacher A might plan a visual and auditory component, while Teacher B plans a tactile/kinesthetic component.	Ensures that all learning modalities are incorporated into instruction	Assumes that teachers will tolerate activity in the lesson
Parallel	Class is broken into two heterogeneous groups. Each teacher takes a group.	Increased participation rates due to smaller group size Effective for limited materials	Requires equal expertise if used for direct content delivery

TABLE P2.1 A Synopsis of Co-Teaching Models—cont'd

	DESCRIPTION	PROS	CONS
Complementary skills	Teacher A focuses on curriculum. Teacher B focuses on access or complementary skills through mini-lessons or input.	Sets up clear expectation that specialized instruction will be provided in general education setting	May slow down pacing
Adapting	Teacher A leads, while Teacher B wanders the room, providing adaptations as needed.	Very little co-planning time Individualized accommodations	Instructional changes are superficial rather than foundational

CHAPTER 4

The Duet Model

The Duet Model is, unarguably, the best model for students. In this model, Teacher A and Teacher B share everything. Right from the beginning there is a sense that the students are "ours" rather than "yours" or "mine." Although this model embraces the unique skills and talents that each teacher brings, it does not expect roles and responsibilities to be delineated based on job title. Both teachers fully collaborate to meet the needs of all students.

> *Right from the beginning there is a sense that the students are "ours" rather than "yours" or "mine."*

At a Glance

Teachers in the Duet Model start by spending time together designing the curriculum for the course. If the curriculum is predetermined, then the teachers review it together, making professional decisions about areas of emphasis and timing. The collaborative process continues as they work to design specific instructional objectives, activities, and assessment tools. The specialist weaves her expertise and the needs of targeted students into the plan they are designing. Planning together requires a significant time investment before the school year begins so that the first day of school finds them ready to present as co-teachers to their class.

Once instruction has begun, Teacher A and Teacher B are usually indistinguishable to students and community visitors. Both teachers take turns with leading the instruction, with supporting individual students, and handling the daily classroom management tasks. An educated observer will

Ms. Trenton, a third-year ELL teacher, and Mrs. Ashland, a veteran fourth-grade teacher, have been assigned to co-teach a language arts block together in the fall. Mrs. Ashland's class will have five students who are receiving English Language services. They are currently functioning on different levels of language acquisition. Ms. Trenton has provided pull-out services to the fourth grade in the past and is somewhat familiar with their language arts curriculum. Their principal has arranged for them to receive two days of stipend money to collaborate in the summer so that they can kick the year off in a highly integrated fashion.

Mrs. Ashland takes the lead in planning by reviewing the current curriculum map and sharing her thoughts about priorities. Ms. Trenton describes the specific needs of the targeted students and suggests areas that will lend themselves well to meeting these needs. They agree that they will use a mixture of co-teaching models, depending on the content and the progress of the students, with flexibility as a key operating principle. The partners look at fiction and nonfiction books that will be culturally sensitive and are available on a variety of reading levels, and discuss writing prompts and strategies that will engage language learners.

By the end of their second planning day, both teachers have a sense of their roles and responsibilities, have brainstormed numerous teaching ideas, and are excited about working together.

notice that the specialist may be more inclined to restate, clarify, adapt, and use specialized instructional techniques than the general educator, but it is usually a subtle difference. The general education teacher may appear to be more knowledgeable about the content, able to add depth to examples, and easily generate acceleration activities. Even with these potential differences, there is still a clear feeling in the Duet Model classroom that this is a shared class.

The Duet Model incorporates many of the other models of co-teaching. Table 4.1 shows the variety of ways teachers using the Duet Model work together throughout the course of a week. Within this plan, the partners have included the Speak and Add Model, the Parallel Model, the Skill Groups Model, the Complementary Skills

TABLE 4.1: Duet Model Unit Plan

DAY 1	DAY 2	DAY 3	DAY 4	DAY 5
OBJECTIVES	**OBJECTIVES**	**OBJECTIVES**	**OBJECTIVES**	**OBJECTIVES**
Define the elements of plot: setting, rising action, climax, denouement/ falling action. Recognize these elements of plot in an oral story told by someone else	Understand and identify plot elements and contextual clues within the Sherlock Holmes story assigned.	Analyze a complete short story based on careful observation; reach conclusions using imagination and information about person(s) observed.	Write a complete short story based on careful observation, including all story elements.	Analyze short story for each plot element assigned.
PROCESS	**PROCESS**	**PROCESS**	**PROCESS**	**PROCESS**
Mrs. K leads with definitions and examples of setting, rising action, climax, denouement/ falling action. Mr. T. puts chart on overhead. Students will be required to take notes on these elements. Guide students in Symbolic Summary. 🧩 Class breaks into two groups to develop personal stories with all the elements, and then tell partners. Debrief whole group—Mr. T. leads	Mr. T leads Board Relay 🧩 warm-up to review elements. Mrs. K presents Holmes stories and assigns reading. Mr. T integrates use of Highlighter Tape. 🧩 Students work individually while both teachers roam. Work in cooperative groups (Group B configurations) to compare elements and justify choices.	Warm-Up Question: If we didn't pay attention to the world and the people in it, what would life be like? Mrs. K leads discussion about Sherlock Holmes' beliefs about observations. Mr. T— Connection Collection 🧩 Students complete graphic organizer—Mr. T to model as Mrs. K. leads. Homework: Observe a stranger in a public setting and jot down observations.	Direct students to compose an imaginative short story based on the facts gathered on the stranger observed for homework. Mrs. K. to model one graphic plan example, Mr. T to share a different way of planning. Both teachers wander and support as students write. Near end of lesson, Mr. T will direct students to review and color code their story elements.	Split class into two groups. Students first describe what they observed, then present their stories, while the rest of the group listens for story elements (use author stools). Facilitate debate/ discussion if different opinions arise about elements, such as the climax. Mr. T to assign Text Message Exit Slips. 🧩

🧩 See Appendix A for a detailed explanation of this instructional strategy.

Model, and have switched the instructional lead several times. This is only possible because they have the time and the skills to communicate regularly and effectively about how to meet the needs of the students in their shared class.

Intense collaboration continues after the instructional phase. Both teachers are involved in assessing all students. This may take the form of turn taking with paper grading, splitting assessment responsibilities based on interests and skills, or sitting side-by-side to grade each student. No matter how the workload is divided, weighty decisions are shared. Consensus is reached so that final grades and reports are viewed by parents and students as a unified decision. Conferencing with parents and students is done by Teacher A and Teacher B, and together they will design the next learning steps for students.

Mr. Hayden and Mrs. Mohagen have recently begun their first year of co-teaching Algebra I. Mr. Hayden, a veteran math specialist, is enthusiastic about developing new skills. Mrs. Mohagen, a highly skilled special education teacher, had some trepidation about co-teaching. She worried about being viewed as an aide by the classroom teacher. But their experience is turning out differently. Mr. Hayden embraces the skills that Mrs. Mohagen has in specially designed instruction. In fact, the differentiation in the classroom is working so well that they have decided to tackle the chapter tests that have been used by the department for the last few years.

After several hours of painstaking work, they have developed a test that allows students to choose which problems to complete, yet doesn't allow students to avoid challenging word problems altogether. They have formatted the test in a way that will work for the students in their Duet Model class that have visual perception problems and fine motor difficulties. After administering and grading the assessment, Mr. Hayden says "It was a lot of work to design the test, but it worked so well for the students. We've decided to keep at it throughout this year and next until we have differentiated assessments that we like for each unit."

Roles and Responsibilities

The Responsibilities Checklist (discussed in Chapter Two) for a Duet Model collaboration between Mrs. Kelleher, a general education teacher, and Mr. Thompson, a special education teacher, is shown in Table 4.2:

TABLE 4.2: Collaborative Teaching Responsibilities Checklist—Duet

WHO WILL BE RESPONSIBLE FOR:	MRS. KELLEHER (GEN. ED)	MR. THOMPSON (SP. ED)	SHARED	COMMENTS
Identifying goals and objectives for the course?			X	
Designing individualized objectives for the targeted students?			X	
Planning instructional activities to achieve the goals?			X	
Selecting and organizing instructional materials?			X	
Teaching specific class content?			X	
Teaching study skills and learning strategies?			X	
Collecting data on student performance?			X	
Establishing and implementing grading procedures?			X	
Establishing and implementing a classroom management plan?			X	
Maintaining home contact?			X	
Modifying curriculum and materials as necessary?			X	
Designing tests, homework, and other assignments?			X	
Providing individual assistance to students?			X	

TABLE 4.2: Collaborative Teaching Responsibilities Checklist—Duet—cont'd

WHO WILL BE RESPONSIBLE FOR:	MRS. KELLEHER (GEN. ED)	MR. THOMPSON (SP. ED)	SHARED	COMMENTS
Taking care of daily routines (for example, attendance and lunch counts)?			X	
Directing paraeducators, parent volunteers, or other support personnel?			X	
Communicating to all appropriate parties regarding the targeted students?			X	

These two teachers agreed that they would share all of the major responsibilities for their co-taught class. The Duet Model is the only model in which all of the responsibilities on the checklist are likely to be shared. However, in practice, there were many situations where it made sense for one to take a lead role. For example, Mr. Thompson has more extensive experience in writing IEPs. To save time, he generated ideas for student objectives on his own, and then discussed these with Mrs. Kelleher to get her input. Mrs. Kelleher has a wealth of content resources—books, websites, articles, and activities—and so it made sense for her to guide the brainstorming of ideas for teaching the content. But Mr. Thompson has a personal passion for sports and nutrition, so he is likely to take the lead if this topic arises in the curriculum. And Mrs. Kelleher has a daughter who has been diagnosed with visual perception difficulties, so she has learned a great deal about that particular challenge and how to address it in a classroom setting. Together, the two teachers blend their knowledge and skills to provide the best instructional experience possible.

Pros and Cons

In an effective Duet Model classroom, the benefits of co-teaching are maximized. Every benefit described in Chapter Two is present in the Duet Model classroom because both teachers work so closely together in all phases of the instructional cycle. A Duet Model team might very well qualify for what Warren Bennis and Pat Ward Biederman call "Great Groups." In their book *Organizing Genius: The Secrets of Creative Collaboration*, they describe Great Groups as people with similar interests who create something together that is not possible on their own. They "can be a goad, a check, a sounding board and a source of inspiration" (1997, 7) for each other that can lead to successful synergy. They work so well together that they create a classroom filled with possibilities and achievements.

What happens in the Duet Model that makes it so powerful? Differentiation is a constant, comprehensive component of instruction. The specialist identifies the needs of targeted students during the initial planning phases. Teachers formulate units with these needs in mind from the very beginning, rather than attempting to integrate these needs after the fact. Day-to-day changes are quickly discussed and agreed on by the teaching partners so that differentiation is flexible and formative. The specialists also brings their unique assessment perspective to the design of projects and products that will provide the team with necessary assessment information. Because the team spends so much time together, it is easy for them to plan for and provide the differentiation students need to be successful.

Professional growth in a Duet Model classroom is extensive. When two teachers work so closely together it is inevitable that they will learn from each other. The general educator gains knowledge about the specialty of his or her teammate. If co-teaching with a gifted education specialist, that knowledge might include simple methods for compacting the curriculum. If co-teaching with an ELL specialist, the classroom teacher might gain knowledge about emphasizing cognates when introducing vocabulary terms. Not only do these new skills assist the classroom teacher in working with targeted students, but these skills also invariably generalize to improving instructional results for all students. Professional growth for the specialist occurs in the content depth and breadth they acquire from working closely with the content expert—the general educator. The pre-service training for most specialists does not delve deeply into any single content area—instead it usually provides a quick survey. The Duet Model experience offers the specialist time and support to expand their content knowledge. This knowledge then becomes transportable, moving with them into encounters they have with students in other co-taught classrooms or in self-contained and resource room settings.

The intensity of the Duet Model results in one major difficulty—time. An enormous amount of time is necessary for the Duet Model to work: time for two teachers to plan together, teach together, and follow-up together. With time already in short supply in our schools, the time demands of this model make it difficult to use. Realistically, the Duet Model is only manageable when the specialist is co-teaching with one teacher, or two at the most. Teachers and administrators must be highly committed to co-planning and willing and able to set it as a top priority. Distractions and "take backs" must be minimized. For example, specialists report that they are occasionally pulled from co-taught instruction to cover for a teacher who is absent. This type of take back undermines the value of the Duet Model and is likely to lead to teacher hesitance to participate. Instead of minimizing the time Duet Model teachers have together, the school administrator must fiercely protect their collaboration.

GUIDING QUESTIONS WHEN CONSIDERING THE DUET MODEL

- Do we have adequate common time to fully share the planning and assessment phases?
- Are we truly willing to view this class as "ours"?
- Do we both feel confident enough with the content knowledge to be equally responsible for the curriculum?

TO SUM UP

- In the Duet Model, both teachers fully share each phase of the instructional cycle. Their skills and experiences are smoothly integrated to provide a tightly integrated approach to teaching.
- Although the Duet Model is the best for students, it is the most time intensive and may not be realistic for specialists who are co-teaching with more than one or two teachers.

CHAPTER 5

Lead and Support Model

For busy specialists, the Lead and Support Model is more practical than the Duet Model. Specialists working with multiple teachers will find it difficult to participate in the amount of collaborative planning that the Duet Model requires. In the Lead and Support Model, much of the advance planning for the year is done by Teacher A, the general educator. This allows Teacher B to focus energy on supporting the classroom teacher and targeted students through the remainder of the instructional cycle.

At a Glance

It is late summer and the school doors will open in two weeks. Mr. Weldon sits hunched over his home computer, examining pacing charts and curriculum maps. This year he will be co-teaching his seventh-grade English/Language Arts class with Mrs. Lee, a literacy specialist. He wonders how the pacing will be affected by her presence and a heavy proportion of struggling readers. Will she want to add so many supportive strategies that he isn't able to cover his content? He sets his worries aside and plans on holding high expectations for all the students to succeed within the time they have together. Mr. Weldon sketches out units, projects, and teaching ideas for the first semester.

In the Lead and Support Model, Teacher A does all the up-front planning in isolation. He determines what the course layout will look like, comes up with ideas for units and projects, chooses major assignments and assessments, selects materials and texts—all of the in-depth planning that happens before school starts. Teacher A is purposefully constructing an instructional plan that will lead students to success.

Teacher B begins her collaborative effort after the plan is in place. The teaching partners will meet for a few hours before their first class together to determine roles and responsibilities, discuss classroom management and grading practices, and iron out some details for their first few classes. Additional questions, such as the following, will need to be answered before the first day of school:

- How should we introduce ourselves to the students?

- What routines can Teacher B handle right from the beginning?

- What will be the best seating arrangement to meet the needs of targeted students?

- What adaptations might need to be in place immediately?

As the semester gets under way, both teachers are fully involved in implementing the original plan. At weekly meetings, the partners discuss ideas for adapting the plan, if necessary, to address the needs of targeted students. Teacher B brings her expertise to the table, suggesting supportive strategies that will make the typical approach more accessible. Changes are made and the partners decide who will lead each portion of the lesson. Table 5.1 shows a lesson plan as originally designed by Teacher A, and as adapted after collaborative discussion with Teacher B.

The casual observer in a Lead and Support Classroom will not be able to distinguish the general education teacher from the specialist. Both adults will embrace significant roles during class time, and students will view them as "our teachers." Close examination by professional educators will reveal a tendency for Teacher B to channel her efforts toward supporting the needs of targeted students. This does not translate to hovering, nor to providing obvious

> *Both adults will embrace significant roles during class time, and students will view them as "our teachers."*

TABLE 5.1: Lead and Support Lesson Plan

7th Grade English/Language Arts—Period 5		
Standard: The student builds vocabulary through reading and systematic word study. The student is expected to: Expand vocabulary by reading, listening, and conversing		
ORIGINAL PLAN	CHANGES FOLLOWING COLLABORATION	ROLES
Preview vocabulary for Chapter 3 of "The Giver."	Slightly expanded vocabulary list Application activity— Words in Context	Mrs. Lee will identify additional words. Mr. Weldon will preview. Mrs. Lee will lead activity.
Students work in groups to read Chapter 3.	Heterogeneous groupings for reading Students have highlighter tape to highlight vocabulary	Both teachers wander and collect observational data.
Students discuss what was read, responding to questions on worksheet provided.	Symbols added next to each question on worksheet	Mrs. Lee will adapt worksheet.
	Think-Pair-Share before whole class summary	Mrs. Lee will lead TPS.
Whole class develops a summary of the chapter, using new vocabulary terms.		Mr. Weldon will lead summary discussion. Mrs. Lee will type and project, highlighting key vocabulary.

assistance. Instead, the supports are usually orchestrated in such a way that the whole class benefits from them without being aware of their targeted purpose.

Ongoing formative assessment will assist teachers in determining their next steps. As defined by Popham, "formative assessment is a planned process in which teachers or students use assessment-based evidence to adjust what they are currently doing" (2008, 6). Because the research (Marzano, 2010) so clearly shows the positive effect of instructional feedback and formative assessment, this will be a prime time for Teacher B to ensure that instruction is being accurately tailored to the needs of targeted students. Though Teacher A's original assessment plan will guide them initially, Teacher B will be on the lookout for adjustments. Specialists often have expertise in assessment that is above and beyond that of the general educator. Here is their opportunity to shape the process of assessment so that it is more formative than summative, or as Stiggins et al. (2006, 31) describe, "assessment for learning" rather than "assessment of learning."

Continuous collaboration will help partners to refine and improve the instructional process. The more time they can find to reflect, analyze, and converse, the more effective they will become as co-teachers. And, if these two teachers continue to co-teach with each other the following year, planning will be significantly more efficient.

Specific grading tasks will be shared. At times, it might be reasonable for Teacher A to handle a larger portion of this responsibility, depending on qualifications and expertise with the content. For example, if Teacher B is not certified in the content area, the partners may decide that Teacher A will grade essays and Teacher B will grade multiple choice questions. Whenever possible, they will sit together and grade the work of targeted students so that the skills and knowledge they both hold is brought to bear on deciphering student work.

Roles and Responsibilities

The Responsibilities Checklist for a Lead and Support collaboration will differ depending on the specialty area of Teacher B, and the number of classrooms she is co-teaching (see Table 5.2). General education teachers who display flexibility and understanding will be greatly appreciated by their partners. Remember, it is usually just Teacher B that must move from class to class, co-teaching with multiple partners and personalities, in multiple content areas. Inevitably, this will affect her ability to equally share all responsibilities.

Pros and Cons

The main advantage of the Lead and Support Model is that it saves Teacher B time. For a specialist co-teaching with multiple teachers, this

TABLE 5.2: Collaborative Teaching Responsibilities Checklist—Lead and Support

WHO WILL BE RESPONSIBLE FOR:	TEACHER A	TEACHER B	SHARED	COMMENTS
Identifying goals and objectives for the course?	X			
Designing individualized objectives for the targeted students?			X	
Planning instructional activities to achieve the goals?			X	Start with A's plan
Selecting and organizing instructional materials?			X	
Teaching specific class content?	X			Mostly A
Teaching study skills and learning strategies?		X		
Collecting data on student performance?			X	
Establishing and implementing grading procedures?			X	
Establishing and implementing a classroom management plan?			X	
Maintaining home contact?			X	
Modifying curriculum and materials as necessary?		X		
Designing tests, homework, and other assignments?	X			Mostly A
Providing individual assistance to students?			X	
Taking care of daily routines (for example, attendance and lunch counts)?	X			
Directing paraeducators, parent volunteers, and other support personnel?			X	
Communicating to all appropriate parties regarding the targeted students?		X		Mostly B

time saving is no small matter. By assigning the total responsibility for advance planning to Teacher A, the specialist is freed up to fulfill other responsibilities she has regarding serving targeted students. This often includes individualized planning meetings, paperwork, formal testing, and extensive communication with parents. When Teacher A assumes responsibility for the advance planning, ripple effects may occur in the pool of other responsibilities. As seen in Table 5.2, Teacher B will spend more time adapting or modifying, rather than engaging in original design; more time teaching learning skills related to the content, rather than the content itself.

It is important to note that the other major advantage of this model is that Teacher B is fully engaged in what happens in the classroom. The interplay between teachers and students is active, continuous and totally utilizes both partners' skills. Instruction in the Lead and Support Model is enriched by all that the specialist brings to the room. "Support" does not mean sitting down and watching, being in charge of "administrivia" or adding to the discourse only occasionally. Instead, the "support" component of this model is a rigorous and vigorous approach for infusing specialized instruction into the general education curriculum.

Unfortunately, because Teacher B is not involved in the up-front planning for the year, differentiated instruction may be less comprehensive than desired. Carol Ann Tomlinson, a leading differentiation advocate, believes that the best differentiation happens when teachers have articulated their philosophies and are grounded in a vision of what classrooms could be like if the capacity of each learner was maximized (1999). To develop and articulate this takes talk time. Though many research-based interventions are simple enough that they can be added on the spot, some require extensive dialogue and preparation. Teachers in the Lead and Support Model often catch themselves saying "If only we had set it up differently in the first place!" On a positive note, teachers who continue to work together for several years in a row find this problem diminishing. The specialist can have a lasting influence on how general educators view lesson design. In subsequent years, the general educator—although still planning alone—begins to weave into his unit plans ideas that were brought to the table by Teacher B. Job-embedded professional development has occurred!

GUIDING QUESTIONS WHEN CONSIDERING THE LEAD AND SUPPORT MODEL

- Are we comfortable with one of us taking a greater lead in the planning, with the other suggesting adjustments afterward?
- Can we identify components of instruction for which Teacher B can take the lead, so that she has an opportunity to offer direct instruction to the class?
- Do we have adequate common planning time to make weekly changes to the plan, discuss student progress, and evaluate our co-teaching?
- Do we have ample ideas for differentiation that can be easily woven into our lesson planning?

TO SUM UP

- In the Lead and Support Model, one teacher accepts the primary responsibility for the advanced planning. Once the plan is in place, both teachers share the instruction, assessment, and reteaching.
- The Lead and Support Model provides an opportunity for a specialist to be significantly involved in teaching, even if he or she does not have the time to participate in extensive planning.

CHAPTER 6

Speak and Add Model

One of the simplest approaches to co-teaching, the Speak and Add Model is usually blended in with other models, rather than used as a stand-alone. This model provides Teacher B with the opportunity to become publicly engaged in the classroom, rather than wandering the aisles quietly. Students benefit from two voices, two perspectives, and two teaching styles as Teacher B verbally and visually participates in the lesson.

At a Glance

In the Speak and Add Model, Teacher A is running the class in a fairly normal manner, while Teacher B is jumping in and adding either verbally or visually. Teacher B's goal is to help the targeted students be successful in whole group settings by integrating simple supports. Though the Speak and Add Model occurs mostly during active instruction, teachers will still benefit from discussing it during the planning phase of the instructional cycle. It is critical that partners give each other permission to "jump in"—accept that their lecture may be interrupted for the sake of clarification, or that an on-the-spot visual support might require an extra minute. If teachers agree up front that this is a valuable method for strengthening instruction, then neither teacher will be flustered or frustrated when it occurs unexpectedly.

> *It is critical that partners give each other permission to "jump in"—accept that their lecture may be interrupted for the sake of clarification, or that an on-the-spot visual support might require an extra minute.*

In this tenth-grade American history class, students are preparing for a required essay. The co-teaching partners have discussed the general plan, but specific details for today's lesson haven't been reviewed. Teacher B will still be able to keep actively engaged in the class by using the Speak and Add Model.

Teacher A: Today we are going to develop our writing plans for our essays comparing tolerance in colonial America to contemporary America. You have scrap paper on your desk. We are going to give you one minute of quiet time to jot down any ideas you have about tolerance in either time period.

Teacher B: It might help to think back to the video we watched on Tuesday.

Teacher A: Now talk for a few minutes in your groups about what you remembered.

Teacher B: I'll start the timer on the screen so that you can monitor your time and make sure everyone has a chance to share. [The allotted time passes.]

Teacher A: Let's hear what you have.

Teacher B: I'll type your ideas into our class notes on the website. When we are finished with our list, we can go back and I'll highlight in green the ideas you think are most important.

Teacher A: Monique, please share one thing your group thought was relevant to the issue of tolerance in either colonial America or contemporary America.

Monique: We felt that someone is always trying to be on top, be in power, and needing to put others down to get there and stay there.

Teacher B: That's an important theme—power. Can you give me a specific example?

As you review this dialogue, you can see that Teacher B is looking for ways to add to the instruction to benefit struggling students. As shown in Table 6.1, there are almost an unlimited number of ways that a teacher might strengthen the general instruction, such as those shown in Table 6.1.

In effective co-teaching, both teachers embrace the benefits of swapping the roles of Teacher A and Teacher B occasionally. Rather than the specialist only serving as Teacher B, there may be times when she is leading the lecture and the general educator takes on Teacher B tasks. By switching roles, both teachers have the

TABLE 6.1: Speak and Add Examples

TEACHER A	TEACHER B
Lecturing	Demonstrating effective note taking on board, overhead projector, or computer/LCD projector
Giving directions	Writing directions on board in a manner effective for students with visual perception difficulties
Leading a discussion with students	Capturing student thoughts in a graphic organizer on the board or on a website such as www.bubbl.us
Using a term that is unfamiliar to students	Adding a definition or rephrasing
Lecturing	Asking a higher level, analytic, evaluative, or creative question
Introducing new concepts to class	Noticing confusion, jumps in and asks a clarifying question
Discussing a controversial subject	Debating on-the-spot to model to students how to work through conflict, support your opinion, agree to disagree
Reading a lengthy piece of text aloud	Sharing the read-aloud to vary vocal qualities and maintain student interest
Lecturing	Adding anecdotes and connections to foster comprehension
Using terminology that may be new to some students	Displaying a synonym website on the projector such as www.visuwords.com
Asking questions of students	Collecting data on student participation levels

opportunity to view students from a new perspective. This enhanced perspective provides them with additional insight when making instructional decisions.

After the instructional phase, co-teachers may share additional responsibilities for assessment, grading, and re-teaching. As mentioned previously, the Speak and Add Model is very rarely used by itself. Co-teaching is best if both adults are more fully utilized. However, this model may be a stepping stone, a starting place for moving into more comprehensive models. For example, there are times when a paraeducator with little content experience may be assigned to a classroom to support a student with disabilities. Due to their lack of content confidence, an assumption might be made that co-teaching is not possible, and the paraeducator may end up spending most of her time sitting in the back next to the targeted student. In this case, the Speak and Add Model is a wonderful way to begin expanding the role of the paraeducator while simultaneously broadening and deepening the supports available to all students in the class. Disturbingly, it is sometimes the highly trained specialist who is found sitting in the back, underutilized. Again, the Speak and Add Model might serve as a necessary stepping stone to lead them to more worthwhile involvement.

Roles and Responsibilities

If this model is used by itself, then the Responsibilities Checklist might look like that shown in Table 6.2. More often, teachers integrate this model with several others to create the best co-teaching design for their students.

Pros and Cons

The interplay between two teachers in the Speak and Add Model requires very little planning time. This simplicity is what makes it a popular model with busy educators. Other benefits, though, make it a model that administrators should encourage all teams to adopt as part of their co-teaching kaleidoscope.

TABLE 6.2: Collaborative Teaching Responsibilities Checklist—Speak and Add

WHO WILL BE RESPONSIBLE FOR:	TEACHER A	TEACHER B	SHARED	COMMENTS
Identifying goals and objectives for the course?	X			
Designing individualized objectives for the targeted students?			X	
Planning instructional activities to achieve the goals?	X			
Selecting and organizing instructional materials?			X	
Teaching specific class content?	X			
Teaching study skills and learning strategies?		X		Informally
Collecting data on student performance?			X	
Establishing and implementing grading procedures?	X			
Establishing and implementing a classroom management plan?	X			B may help with implementation
Maintaining home contact?			X	
Modifying curriculum and materials as necessary?			X	
Designing tests, homework, and other assignments?	X			.
Providing individual assistance to students?			X	
Taking care of daily routines (for example, attendance and lunch counts)?	X			
Directing paraeducators, parent volunteers, or other support personnel?	X			
Communicating to all appropriate parties regarding the targeted students?		X		Mostly B

Student attention is heightened in a classroom where vocal qualities, teaching styles, and personalities change frequently—especially during long blocks of instructional time. Rather than becoming overly familiar with one teaching style to the point of tuning it out, students can be unexpectedly presented with a new view, a new sound, or a new perspective. Just as sports fans closely watch a basketball game to see which team will grab the ball next, students pay close attention to the interplay between their co-teachers.

> *Student attention is heightened in a classroom where vocal qualities, teaching styles, and personalities change frequently—especially during long blocks of instructional time.*

Student frustration is diminished in a Speak and Add Model classroom. In a traditional setting, a student who doesn't understand an unfamiliar term or a complex direction has a few unappealing options. The student may proceed incorrectly, disengage due to frustration or embarrassment, wait until much later (out of context) to ask for clarification, or interrupt the lesson to request help. In the co-taught setting, Teacher B is always on the lookout to prevent this scenario from happening. By anticipating confusing terms, presenting information visually, rephrasing and questioning, Teacher B proactively supports struggling students.

Perhaps the most important benefit of the Speak and Add Model is that anyone can do it. Teacher B does not need to have content expertise to use this model. This model is a perfect fit for when a specialist or a paraeducator is assigned to co-teach in a content area for which she is not adequately trained. For example, an ELL teacher may be assigned to co-teach in a high school geometry class to support students who are still acquiring basic English language skills. Although she is an expert in teaching English to speakers of other languages, her command of geometry may be weak. She may remember squeaking by in her high school geometry class and have great trepidation about assuming an active role in the classroom. By understanding the nature of the Speak and Add Model, she will be more comfortable and willing to interact with the students and the content. Eventually, her geometry knowledge will grow and the partners can expand their view of co-teaching to include other models.

The simplicity of this model makes it attractive as a first step into co-teaching for busy specialists. However, using only this model can lead to a significant problem. If the specialist is always expected to be the one who "adds" rather than leads, her skills will be vastly underutilized. Once a role is established, it can set up patterns of behavior and attitude between the teachers. It may be very difficult for the specialist to break out of this role and share fully in the instructional process.

GUIDING QUESTIONS WHEN CONSIDERING THE SPEAK AND ADD MODEL

- Are we both comfortable with the feeling of interruption that occurs when one teacher jumps in to make a comment?
- Can we develop a signaling system to let each other know when not to interrupt?
- Can we identify opportunities in which Teacher B will take the lead, so that Teacher A can be free to observe student reactions to the lesson, assess informally and then jump in to add supportive comments or visuals?
- What else can we do to ensure that Teacher B is not underutilized?

TO SUM UP

- In the Speak and Add Model, one teacher assumes responsibility for leading instruction while the other adds verbally or visually to enhance the learning. Teachers may exchange these roles throughout the lesson, flexibly supporting the needs of students by jumping in with additional explanations, graphics, verbal emphasis, illustrative anecdotes, or other clarifications.
- The Speak and Add Model is a clear choice for co-teachers with limited planning time and for specialists who are not familiar with the curricular content. However, this model is best utilized in conjunction with other, more in-depth models of co-teaching.

CHAPTER 7

Skill Groups Model

Another powerful way to co-teach is by using the Skill Groups Model. Of all the models, this one most clearly expects teachers to provide instruction at a variety of readiness levels within a single lesson.

At a Glance

Ms. Silva, a board of education member, has made arrangements to visit co-teaching classrooms in several of the district's schools. While she has been a vocal advocate for inclusive practices, she wants to see for herself what co-teaching looks like in action.

Her first stop is a fourth-grade class, co-taught between Mrs. Eley and Mrs. Harrington, a specialist in gifted education. She enters the classroom expecting to find Mrs. Harrington working with a small group of advanced learners at a back table. Instead, she finds a room buzzing with activity. Some students are at their desks, others on the floor, and several are at standing work stations. Some students are working quietly while others are engaged in lively discussion with peers. Both teachers are wandering the room, monitoring student work and facilitating learning. The classroom teacher excuses herself momentarily from the students and hands Ms. Silva a lesson plan to peruse (see Table 7.1).

After the observation, the co-teachers have an opportunity to debrief with Ms. Silva. Mrs. Harrington describes their philosophy: "Whenever possible, we try to design whole group instruction which subtly addresses various instructional levels, rather than separating a small group of students. By doing this, we can expose all the students to higher order thinking skills and challenging activities. Sometimes we are pleasantly surprised to see a less advanced student rise to the challenge!"

TABLE 7.1: Skill Groups Lesson Plan

Objective: Students will be able to generate ideas for creative writing	
GENERAL APPROACH TO LESSON	**ADAPTATIONS TO RAISE COMPLEXITY**
Mrs. H. will use www.RedKid.net, a sign generator website, to grab attention with whole class Mrs. E. will provide a mini-lesson introducing Pen the Tale 🧩—a strategy for mixing and matching different characters, actions and writing formats Mrs. H. will model her thinking aloud for an unusual combination Students will work independently or with peers to Pen the Tale Mrs. H. will develop/provide a worksheet for students to add to writing journal	Pen the Tale will include some challenging formats that have not been introduced in the fourth-grade curriculum Mrs. H. will set up and guide a computer station with a synonym generator website (www.visuwords.com)
	ADAPTATIONS TO SIMPLIFY COMPLEXITY
	Students will be directed toward choosing simpler combinations and formats Restickable dots will add tactile interaction Multiple ideas will be recorded in a journal prior to deciding which to write about

🧩 See Appendix A

The Skill Groups Model asks the co-teachers to take a heterogeneous group of students and divide it into two or three more homogeneous ability-based groups for the purposes of planning and instruction. Sometimes these groups are physically separated, moving into different areas of the room and participating in different activities. But sometimes, as in the example above, the students work in a whole-group environment, with various levels seamlessly woven into the whole-group structure. The whole-group option allows all students to benefit from the expertise of two adults and be exposed to various instructional levels and strategies.

Teachers occasionally decide that students will benefit most from being divided into small groups based on readiness level. This decision is usually based on the recognition that one or more of the groups needs intense, focused instruction from a teacher. When partners make this decision, it is extremely important that the instruction they design for all groups is engaging. Problems are sure to arise if one group is involved in a stimulating, hands-on experience while the others are offered worksheets or humdrum review activities.

The following questions can guide teachers in choosing between the two options:

- Are students expected to show mastery at the end of this lesson? If so, do we need intense, focused, small-group instruction to accomplish that?

- Does the lesson allow for lots of individual work time naturally? Will we be able to wander and support individual students working at their own levels?

- Can we design a whole group lesson that includes strategies for simplifying the complexity while simultaneously including strategies for increasing the complexity?

- Have we committed to any individualized objectives that can only be addressed in a smaller group setting?

Roles and Responsibilities

The Skill Groups Model is often a component of the Duet Model. During their collaborative planning time, the teachers determine that a specific objective will be most effectively attained by addressing multiple instructional levels. This decision leads the teachers to confer about the benefits of separate small groups versus a large group approach. After reaching a conclusion, the partners split the responsibilities.

The Skill Groups Model can also be used without the in-depth planning required in the Duet Model. When a specialist has limited time for planning or for providing services in the general education classroom, the teammates might agree that the Skill Groups Model will be used for each of her visits. For example, a specialist in gifted education may be scheduled to co-teach in a specific classroom once or twice a week. She will need to ensure that her time provides a "bang"—a very direct, impactful lesson for the targeted students. Her responsibilities will be more limited than if she was able to fully share the role of teacher. Table 7.2 shows common responsibilities for partners using the Skill Groups Model.

TABLE 7.2: Collaborative Teaching Responsibilities Checklist—Skill Groups

WHO WILL BE RESPONSIBLE FOR:	TEACHER A	TEACHER B	SHARED	COMMENTS
Identifying goals and objectives for the course?	X			
Designing individualized objectives for the targeted students?			X	
Planning instructional activities to achieve the goals?	X			
Selecting and organizing instructional materials?			X	
Teaching specific class content?			X	
Teaching study skills and learning strategies?		X		Focus on needs of targeted students
Collecting data on student performance?			X	
Establishing and implementing grading procedures?	X			
Establishing and implementing a classroom management plan?	X			B will help with implementation
Maintaining home contact?			X	
Modifying curriculum and materials as necessary?			X	B to focus on targeted students
Designing tests, homework, and other assignments?			X	B to focus on targeted students
Providing individual assistance to students?			X	
Taking care of daily routines (for example, attendance and lunch counts)?	X			
Directing paraeducators, parent volunteers, or other support personnel?	X			
Communicating to all appropriate parties regarding the targeted students?		X		Mostly B

Pros and Cons

One of the key components of differentiated instruction is readiness level. Any class will contain students functioning at a range of levels. The dedicated teacher, the teacher who has a desire to move all students forward, recognizes that instruction must accommodate multiple instructional levels. As a solo teacher, this is a laudable but difficult goal. As a co-teacher, this goal becomes reachable. Two adults, purposefully constructing and implementing lessons together, can provide students with instruction catered to their current readiness levels. The Skill Groups Model is the only co-teaching model that is clearly defined by this goal.

Specialists who are spread thinly across multiple classrooms appreciate the focus of the Skill Groups Model. Rather than being fully involved in all aspects of educating a particular class of students, the specialist can concentrate

> *Two adults, purposefully constructing and implementing lessons together, can provide students with instruction catered to their current readiness levels.*

his or her skills on meeting the needs of targeted students while still having an influence on instruction for students who have not been labeled. In the previous example, Mrs. Harrington has suggested a writing activity that will challenge the students identified as gifted while also enriching the writing experience for all the students in the class. At other times, she may design an activity for a small, more homogeneous group of students who are at an advanced readiness stage with the specific content of the day. This group will be composed primarily of labeled students, but will likely include others who are ready to be challenged. While the specialist is providing a stimulating small-group lesson to her group, the other groups are also receiving interesting leveled instruction and activities.

Another benefit arises from the Skill Groups Model when co-teachers use the whole-group option. Because targeted students are not pulled aside into a homogeneous group, the fact that they are "different"—struggling, learning English, and so forth—is deemphasized. They are less likely to experience embarrassment or a sense of isolation than when they are physically separated. Therefore, many co-teachers make it their goal to mix the two approaches as much as possible.

The most significant risk of this model arises from the use of small, separate groups. A sense of tracking can occur if the small groups always have the same membership, and the specialist is always the one who works with the targeted group. Students may voice complaints about being pulled aside, about being embarrassed, or about not having access to the activities other students are experiencing. Co-teachers will want to be sensitive to student perceptions and feelings when designing small groups.

An additional risk to only using small groups—the rest of the class is less likely to benefit from the specialist's expertise. Because specialists have a bounty of skills that can enrich learning for all students, co-teachers will want to develop ways to spread the wealth.

GUIDING QUESTIONS WHEN CONSIDERING THE SKILL GROUPS MODEL

- Are we both comfortable with a moderate level of noise in the room as multiple groups are engaged, perhaps in different activities?
- Can we think of ways to avoid having students feel like they are in "the dummies" group?
- Would we design the whole lesson together, or each take on the responsibility of designing for specific groups?
- Do we have strategies for quickly moving students into groups so that time is not wasted?
- Are there natural spaces in the room that lend themselves to dividing up into groups?

TO SUM UP

- In the Skill Groups Model, teachers place a strong emphasis on differentiation. Instructional design incorporates multiple readiness levels so that student needs are met.

- Teachers must carefully design the levels of instruction so that students who struggle are not embarrassed by easier work. Teachers can take proactive steps to develop a classroom culture that respects individual learning differences.

CHAPTER 8

Station Model

Note Found in Mailbox:

Laura,

These five kids are really struggling with decimals—conversion from cm to dm to m. Can you do a station with them on Wednesday?

Luke, Stacia, Tremaine, Jesse, Carin

Nancy

At a Glance

In every heterogeneous classroom, there will be a handful of students that occasionally need extra direct, intensive instruction. The Station Teaching Model allows for this intensity by pulling those students off to the side of the room—a station—so that the teacher can focus instruction on very specific areas of need. In the past, this level of support would have been accomplished by pulling the students out of the general education classroom and serving them in another setting. Speech therapy, special education, gifted education, Title 1, ELL—all of these services have been provided in a pull-out location. The Station Teaching Model replicates the advantages of this focused approach without as many of the disadvantages.

Partners begin by identifying a specific skill deficit or learning need that several students share. If the partners are co-teaching daily, this need will be identified through daily dialogue and reflection about the lessons. If partners are co-teaching less frequently, one or the other of the teachers might notice and express his or her concern, as in the note at the beginning of this chapter. After the need has been identified, either of the teachers can design an instructional experience for that group of students. Often the assumption is that the specialist will work with the targeted students. Though this makes sense most of the time, it may not always be the best solution. For example, if an ELL specialist is co-teaching for the first time in a high school algebra class, his content expertise in algebra may not match that of the math teacher. In this case, it might be best if the algebra teacher takes on the station instruction while the ELL teacher monitors the other students performing independent work.

While co-teaching in Denver Public Schools, my colleague and I designed an effective technique for determining station participation in our middle school math class. At the beginning of a workbook or practice activity, students were provided with strips of green, yellow, and red sticky dots. We directed students to place a dot next to each problem as they completed it. A legend on the board explained:

Green = I got it! Very confident. I am sure it's right.

Yellow = Not sure. Maybe it's right, maybe it's not.

Red = Don't understand. Pretty sure I got it wrong.

Mr. Mediatore, the certified math teacher, manned a station off to the side of the room. As a special educator, I wandered the room while the students were working. Whenever three or four students placed a red dot next to the same problem, they would be sent to the station to work with the math teacher for a few minutes. As they finished up, another group with similar confusion would be sent over for help at the station. Not only did this strategy encourage students to reflect on their work in progress, but it also provided an immediate and flexible way to identify students who would benefit from station teaching.

In elementary and early middle school grades, teachers will usually decide which students will participate in the station activity. As students age, teachers might allow them to self-select. The co-teachers might announce: "For the next 15 minutes, you may work on your plate tectonics RAFT assignment by yourself or with a partner. Mr. Wilson will be available for questions and guidance. During this same time, Mrs. Bauman will be at the station. Anyone who was absent, or has any questions or confusion about the theory of plate tectonics, can join her at the station."

By allowing students to choose participation at a station, the stigma of being identified as "needy" is reduced. The gathering of students at the station may include students that would otherwise not have been chosen by the teacher—perhaps an advanced student who missed class the day the content was introduced. This variety can lead to more engaging dialogue and participation.

What is happening with the rest of the class while targeted students are at the station? This is an important question for co-teachers to discuss. Targeted students cannot afford to fall behind their peers by being pulled off to the side while new information is being provided to the rest of the class. Nor can teachers afford to slow down pacing while a small group is provided with extra instruction or practice time. Therefore, co-teachers must look for brief periods of time that occur during the week—five to fifteen minutes when stations won't detract from the overall learning goals in the classroom.

Picture a class of thirty students. A small group of students is working with one of the teachers at a station while the rest of the class might be:

- Getting a head start on a homework assignment

- Sharing their writing with peers

- Working on independent projects

- Receiving supplemental or enrichment material that is not required for mastery

- Taking a test

- Discussing a reading passage in small groups

- Completing a graphic organizer

Formative assessment is a natural part of the station teaching model. As a teacher works with a small, targeted group of students, she can continuously assess their level of understanding and adjust instruction accordingly.

Summative assessment can also be incorporated into the station teaching model. Some students may require accommodations during testing, based on decisions by their teaching team, and agreed to in an IEP, 504 plan, or other learning contract. Historically, students with these kinds of individualized testing plans have been removed from the class to an alternate testing environment. Removing students from the classroom to provide these accommodations in an alternative location may penalize students in unexpected ways. Marilee Sprenger, educator and memory expert, explains that memory is often linked to a learning location (2005). By providing test accommodations for students in the same location where the material was originally learned, students can tap into these location memory links to access the information. Stations allow for most testing accommodations to take place in the classroom setting. For example, if an agreement has been reached that a student needs the test read aloud, one teacher might inform the class that she will be reading the test aloud to anyone who would like to join her at the station. This arrangement meets the needs of the student(s) for whom a legal agreement has been designed, but also addresses the needs of students not identified as having a disability.

> *Stations allow for most testing accommodations to take place in the classroom setting.*

Roles and Responsibilities

The Station Teaching model is only used in conjunction with other co-teaching models to design the ideal instructional approach for a class. Roles and responsibilities throughout the week and semester will vary depending on which other models are utilized. However, while station teaching is occurring, the responsibilities might be divided as shown in Table 8.1.

Pros and Cons

> *If only I could have some extra time with a few of my students to help them understand this.*

> *I know that he would get it if I could just sit down with him and guide him through some extra practice.*

> *Those three kids seem bored, but I don't have the time to do enrichment activities with them.*

TABLE 8.1: Collaborative Teaching Responsibilities Checklist—Station Teaching

WHO WILL BE RESPONSIBLE FOR:	TEACHER A	TEACHER B	SHARED	COMMENTS
Identifying goals and objectives for the course?	X			
Designing individualized objectives for the targeted students?			X	
Planning instructional activities to achieve the goals?	X			B will plan the station activity
Selecting and organizing instructional materials?	X			B will manage materials for the station
Teaching specific class content?	X			
Teaching study skills and learning strategies?		X		Provided at the station
Collecting data on student performance?			X	
Establishing and implementing grading procedures?	X			
Establishing and implementing a classroom management plan?	X			B will manage students at the station
Maintaining home contact?			X	
Modifying curriculum and materials as necessary?			X	
Designing tests, homework, and other assignments?			X	
Providing individual assistance to students?			X	
Taking care of daily routines (for example, attendance and lunch counts)?	X			
Directing paraeducators, parent volunteers, or other support personnel?	X			
Communicating to all appropriate parties regarding the targeted students?			X	

Dedicated teachers often feel frustrated by the time constraints of a traditional classroom. One of the beauties of co-teaching is that time becomes a bit more flexible. Having two adults in a classroom increases the ability to take time with targeted students for focused assistance. This is especially true of the Station Teaching Model. One of the two adults can concentrate his or her attention on tailoring instruction to a few needy students while the other continues to lead the rest of the class.

Caution must be taken when using the Station Teaching Model so that specific students do not begin to feel isolated or embarrassed by being pulled to the station. In the early grades, children may think it a privilege to spend extra time with the teacher. But as children age, their perceptions will change and may cause reluctance. Secondary students may even refuse to go to the station. These types of reactions are understandable and can be preempted by careful adult orchestration.

While the Station Teaching Model is in use, several of the benefits of co-teaching are lost. Students are not receiving two perspectives, two sets of experiences, two voices . . . instead they are receiving only one. In addition, because groups at a station are more homogeneous in skill level, students are not being exposed to the breadth and depth of discussion, modeling, and insight that comes from a heterogeneous experience. Teachers who are mindful of these disadvantages will be sure to blend the Station Teaching Model with other models, rather than use it as their only structure for co-teaching.

GUIDING QUESTIONS WHEN CONSIDERING THE STATION MODEL

- Will any of the other models work to accomplish the same learning goal so that individual students do not need to be separated?
- What type of response will we have when students question being separated? Or show great reluctance to go to the station?
- How often are we comfortable using this model?
- Do we have a space that will work well for a station without becoming a distraction?

TO SUM UP

- The Station Model, used only in conjunction with other models, allows for one teacher to pull a small group of students to a station to provide direct, intense instruction. Participation in the group is flexible and is determined based on similar need for support or enrichment.

- The Station Model should be used with caution. If overused it can establish a sense of separateness among students and teachers.

CHAPTER 9

Learning Style Model

Over the years, much has been published on individual learning styles or preferences (Beninghof, 1998; Carbo, 2009; Dunn and Dunn, 1993). Noted psychologist and researcher Howard Gardner stated: "Education has been the idea of uniform schooling . . . and it's presumed to be fair. Actually, it is the most unfair thing in the world. We have to individuate education, teaching as many children as possible, in as many ways as possible" (1997). The Learning Style Model provides co-teachers with a structure that prompts them to continually infuse multiple modalities into their instruction, so as to teach in as many ways as possible.

At a Glance

The sixth-grade English/Language Arts teachers are wrapping up their biweekly planning session with Mrs. Murphy, an occupational therapist. Mrs. McCoy, one of the general education teachers, is appreciated by her colleagues for always thinking ahead. She mentions that the next unit will be on three-paragraph essay writing and expresses concern that some students may struggle with the attention and endurance needed to meet the benchmark. Mrs. Murphy sees an opportunity to contribute ideas and address the needs of her targeted students. Grabbing a marker, she outlines a graphic organizer for brainstorming visual, auditory, tactile, and kinesthetic ideas. The team begins to generate a variety of ways to approach the learning objective and include all learning styles.

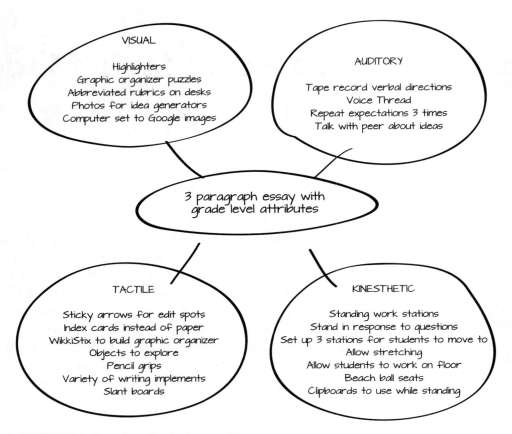

FIGURE 9.1: Learning Style Lesson Ideas

The Learning Style Model begins with a belief that students learn best through a variety of modalities or approaches. Although there has been some disagreement about whether individuals truly have a dominant modality (Willingham, 2009), the good news is that there seems to be consensus about the fact that when we learn through multiple pathways, we are activating more neural connections. This leads to more solid understanding, a deepening of comprehension, and more accessible memories.

Many learning style frameworks have been put forth for teachers to use in their classrooms (Dunn and Dunn, 1993; Carbo, 1994; Silver, Strong, and Perini, 2007; McCarthy, 1996; Gardner, 1993). Each and every one of them provides us with a multifaceted view of learning and wonderful direction for instruction. However, busy teachers often balk at the implementation of more complex models. It is common after a staff development workshop to hear teachers lament, "I like the concept, but who has time to design instruction in so many different ways?" Instead, using just the four perceptual modalities—visual, auditory, tactile, and kinesthetic—seems to be much more doable. Teachers already rely on visual and auditory instructional techniques. This approach simply asks teachers to add two more dimensions to their instruction. Therefore, the Learning Style Model discussed here will focus on the four perceptual modalities, but can easily be expanded to include other facets of learning preference.

Co-teachers who choose to use the Learning Style Model find it helpful to gather information about student learning style preferences. This data provides teachers with information for planning instruction, adjusting teaching on the spot, and guiding students to study strategies that are a good match. As students become aware of their own preferences they can integrate them into their homework routines and begin to advocate for their needs.

A variety of methods exist for identifying student learning styles. Many evaluations that determine special education eligibility contain sections identifying learning strengths and weaknesses. Test results or evaluator comments might indicate an auditory processing problem, tactile defensiveness, or other difficulties. The Learning Style Inventory (Dunn, Dunn, and Price, 1994) and the Reading Style Inventory (Carbo, 1994) were designed to give a comprehensive profile of an individual student's learning strengths and preferences. Both inventories present a series of questions and pictures and ask the student to make a choice from several options. The student's answers lead to a learning style profile, from which appropriate instructional strategies can be determined.

A simpler approach for busy teachers is to use the observation method. Although observation may not yield accurate information in all areas of learning preference, research shows that teachers are highly accurate at determining a student's perceptual modality strength through observation (Dunn, Dunn, and Price, 1994). The Student Learning Style Observation Tool (Worksheet 9.1) can be used as an easy checklist while teachers are getting to know their students at the beginning of the semester (Beninghof, 1998).

To gain full advantage of the Learning Style Model, teachers will want to teach students about learning style theory and how it relates to them. General concepts to share with students include

WORKSHEET 9.1: Student Learning Style Observation Tool

Student Name: _____ **Date:** _____

Teacher: _____

Check the behaviors that you observe the student exhibiting frequently.

VISUAL	AUDITORY
☐ Taking copious notes ☐ Drawing or doodling ☐ Wanting to look at the pictures accompanying text ☐ Needing eye contact to listen well ☐ Choosing visual tasks, such as reading ☐ Closely examining objects and pictures ☐ Commenting on the visual aspects of something	☐ Choosing to listen to audiotapes ☐ Following verbal directions while not appearing to be listening ☐ Showing a preference for music or singing ☐ Showing an interest in oral discussions ☐ Reading aloud to self ☐ Sounding out words ☐ Talking to self

TACTILE	KINESTHETIC
☐ Touching objects on shelves ☐ Fiddling with items in desk ☐ Carrying small objects around in hand ☐ Choosing to work with manipulatives whenever possible ☐ Grabbing items ☐ Playing with pencils and pens	☐ Walking around the room ☐ Standing while working at desk ☐ Jumping out of seat ☐ Using body movements for expression ☐ Enjoying physical education and other movement opportunities ☐ Volunteering to demonstrate or run errands ☐ Acting and playing roles

Source: Beninghof, 1998. Used with permission.

- Everyone learns through all four modalities (visual, auditory, tactile, kinesthetic).

- No single modality is better than the others.

- Teachers have learning style preferences just as students do.

- By interacting with peers, students can learn other ways to approach learning.

- It is fair for teachers to design instruction that may be different for some students so that all students learn successfully.

- All people experience times when instruction does not match their learning preferences, and must learn to cope by seeking and utilizing other learning strategies.

- There are appropriate times and ways for students to advocate for themselves in regard to learning style.

Designing and implementing co-taught lessons with the Learning Style Model usually involves two approaches. The first approach is flexible, on-the-spot enrichment. Partners begin by admitting to each other that there are times when they might fall into a habit of lecturing (auditory) without taking into account other modalities. Partners then give each other permission to jump into a lesson and add an alternate modality as they see fit. For example, one teacher may be following the original plan for peers to discuss a video after viewing it. The second teacher, recognizing that students have been sitting for an extended period of time, jumps in with the "Vote with Your Feet" strategy, asking students to stand and move along an imaginary continuum to express their agreement with a point of view. For this flexible approach to work, both teachers must be comfortable with unexpected shifts, aware of pacing guidelines, and willing to be honest about how it is affecting their instructional flow. When these factors are in place, a wonderful synergy can happen between partners.

The second approach to the Learning Style Model is planned for in advance by building multiple modalities into the original lesson design. Partners may plan this together, or may divide responsibilities, with one planning a visual and auditory component, the other a tactile and kinesthetic component. Specialists usually have more training and experience in multimodality instructional techniques, and thus often take the lead in developing tactile and

TABLE 9.1: Learning Style Lesson Plan

Standard: Create and solve problems that involve multiplication of multi-digit number	
Objective: Students will accurately compute two	
VISUAL—TEACHER A	**AUDITORY—TEACHER A**
Examples on overhead Chart of process steps	Rhythmic chant of process steps
TACTILE—TEACHER B	**KINESTHETIC—TEACHER B**
Puff paint on process worksheet Manipulatives	Students work at board

kinesthetic activities. A Learning Style lesson plan may look like that shown in Table 9.1:

Teachers can also use lesson planning forms required by their district by simply adding four checkboxes marked V, A, T and K, and checking them off to indicate that the plan includes those modalities.

The assessment phase can also incorporate the learning preferences of students. Instead of offering one and only one way to show knowledge and mastery, co-teachers can offer students choices. As long as a rubric is in place that clearly describes the mastery criteria, teachers should be able to fairly and accurately grade a variety of demonstrations of learning. Table 9.2 lists myriad approaches that teachers could pick and choose from in offering students assessment options.

> *Instead of offering one and only one way to show knowledge and mastery, co-teachers can offer students choices.*

Roles and Responsibilities

Roles and responsibilities will depend greatly on whether the partners are taking a formal or informal approach to this model. In a formal approach, Teacher A would take responsibility for planning a visual and auditory approach to the learning objective, while Teacher B would design a tactile and kinesthetic approach. The roles would

TABLE 9.2: Differentiated Assessment Activities and Tools

VISUAL	AUDITORY
Exhibits	Speeches
Posters	Debates
Outlines	Interviews
Patterns	Audio recordings
Creative designs	Questions and answers
Visuals	Oral reports
Graphic organizers	Explanations
Art media	Jokes and riddles
Displays	Storytelling
Charts	Songs or raps
Brochures	Poetry
Illustrations	Jingles and cheers
Cartoons and caricatures	Dramatic interpretations
Photography	

TACTILE	KINESTHETIC
Journals or diaries	Interpretive dance or movement
Written assignments	Role plays
Demonstrations	Simulations
Manipulatives	Field trips
Board games	Pantomime
Sculptures	Physical games
Multimedia presentation	Inventions
Displays	Dramatic interpretation
Experiments	Movement routines
Inventions	Demonstration
Models	Experiments

be clearly defined in the planning and implementation phases. If the partners choose to be more flexible and informal, then both teachers would be responsible for being on constant lookout for appropriate opportunities to augment the lesson with multimodality techniques.

The Learning Styles Model can be easily infused into any of the other models. In fact, it makes good teaching sense that this model be infused into daily classroom instruction, even in solo-taught classes. When a teacher is solo, her goal will be to embed all four modalities by herself—a reachable goal, but challenging. When two teachers share the responsibility, they can easily craft lessons that engage all students. Shared responsibilities are the norm for this model, as shown in Table 9.3.

TABLE 9.3: Collaborative Teaching Responsibilities Checklist—Learning Styles

WHO WILL BE RESPONSIBLE FOR:	TEACHER A	TEACHER B	SHARED	COMMENTS
Identifying goals and objectives for the course?	X			
Designing individualized objectives for the targeted students?			X	
Planning instructional activities to achieve the goals?			X	
Selecting and organizing instructional materials?			X	
Teaching specific class content?			X	
Teaching study skills and learning strategies?		X		
Collecting data on student performance?			X	
Establishing and implementing grading procedures?			X	
Establishing and implementing a classroom management plan?			X	
Maintaining home contact?			X	
Modifying curriculum and materials as necessary?			X	
Designing tests, homework, and other assignments?			X	
Providing individual assistance to students?			X	
Taking care of daily routines (for example, attendance and lunch counts)?	X			
Directing paraeducators, parent volunteers, or other support personnel?	X			
Communicating to all appropriate parties regarding the targeted students?			X	

Pros and Cons

Sensory-rich classrooms activate multiple neural pathways and lead to stronger learning for all students. But the benefits are especially strong for students who struggle. Research suggests that the majority of students who struggle indicate a preference for tactile and kinesthetic learning, and have a tendency toward weaker auditory memory. By incorporating all four of the sensory modalities into the instructional plan for all students, teachers bypass the risks involved in just teaching to students who have strong auditory skills.

Anyone who has cruised a high school hallway, glancing into classrooms as they pass, has seen the frequency of "sit and get" learning. Though not as common in elementary schools, the proportion of seat time grows at an alarming rate as students grow. Ask a group of teachers why this persists in education and you will hear reasons ranging from "If students are moving, they will get out of control" to "We don't have time to do hands-on stuff." And yet, these same teachers will agree that after twenty or so minutes of sitting, students' attention drifts. In the Learning Style Model this doesn't happen. Through carefully orchestrated infusion of movement, teachers are able to maintain student attention and engagement.

> *Sensory-rich classrooms activate multiple neural pathways and lead to stronger learning for all students.*

Key to the success of the Learning Style Model are the words "carefully orchestrated." If teachers are not careful, multimodality instruction can slow down the pacing in the class, result in some classroom management problems, and become fluff. Educator Mike Schmoker uses the term "crayola curriculum" (2001) to refer to hands-on activities that do not have clear, important purpose in achieving the learning goal. Co-teachers will need to engage in thoughtful analysis to determine that their plan for multimodality infusion has a valid pedagogical purpose.

> *Co-teachers will need to engage in thoughtful analysis to determine that their plan for multimodality infusion has a valid pedagogical purpose.*

GUIDING QUESTIONS WHEN CONSIDERING THE LEARNING STYLE MODEL

- Do we have students who seem to need hands-on instruction to deepen their comprehension?
- Do we have an idea bank from which to draw visual, auditory, tactile, and kinesthetic strategies?
- Is one of us more knowledgeable about multimodality teaching strategies?
- Who will be responsible for obtaining the materials that might be necessary? Where can they be stored? Do we have some ideas for quick distribution and collection?
- What classroom management techniques will we use to ensure that activity levels are not disruptive to the learning process?

TO SUM UP

- In the Learning Style Model, co-teachers plan instructional and assessment activities that address the wide range of learning modalities found in a heterogeneous classroom. Students will be involved in visual, auditory, tactile, and kinesthetic experiences—creating an active (and sometimes noisy!) classroom environment.
- This model is especially beneficial for students who struggle with language, either because of a learning disability or second language acquisition. Instead of the traditional auditory and visual, language-based approach to instruction, students receive a richer exposure through the added hands-on experience.

CHAPTER 10

Parallel Teaching Model

Aptly named, the Parallel Teaching Model divides one large group of students into two smaller, heterogeneous groups for the purpose of instruction. Each teacher works with half the class. This model can be used for an entire class period, but is most often used for brief application exercises because it allows greater opportunity for student participation.

At a Glance

In Exhibit 10.1, two middle school teachers use the Parallel Model during a writing lesson, allowing them to connect more directly within a smaller group.

In the Parallel Teaching Model co-teachers split a class into two heterogeneous groups of students. Both teachers then teach the same content, in the same way, at the same time. Because both teachers will teach the same content in the same way, planning is best accomplished through collaboration. This ensures that both partners will feel comfortable with the content and the method. This also allows them to discuss any classroom management issues that might arise due to doubling the activity in the same space. But it is also possible for Teacher A to plan the lesson by himself and then provide a copy to Teacher B for implementation. In this case, it is essential that Teacher B is competent and confident enough with the content to step into this role without much discussion.

During instruction, each teacher will be carefully monitoring the comprehension within her group. Based on this continuous monitoring, on-the-spot changes to instruction might become necessary. When this happens, the path of the two groups might diverge. One group might spend more time sharing connections, reviewing key directions, practicing skills, or

EXHIBIT 10.1: Lesson Plan for Wednesday, 7th Grade ELA, Mr. Asham and Mrs. Collins

Objective:

Students will apply the six trait writing process to the development of a persuasive argument.

Each student will:

- Apply the six traits of writing (Ideas and Content, Organization, Voice, Sentence Fluency, Word Choice, and Conventions)
- Identify the components of a personal letter
- Apply persuasive writing techniques to create a persuasive apology letter

Materials Needed:

Notes and handouts of the six traits of writing, laptop and projector, markers, butcher paper, journals

Anticipatory Set:

Students will split into two groups for Group Graffiti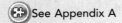 activity. Graffiti topic will be "excuses." Each student will have a marker. Each teacher will direct students to draw graffiti (or tagging) about the concept of "excuses" on their butcher paper. Groups will present briefly to each other after five minutes.

Lesson:

1. Students will return to desks and choose a famous person or character who has done something wrong.

2. Teacher will project example on board of apology/excuse letter from Brittney Spears. "Dear Fans, Oops, I did it again . . ."

3. Students will highlight the components of a well-written letter . . .

See Appendix A

generating creative applications, thus taking longer to accomplish the original learning goal. Effective co-teachers try to synchronize before and during implementation, but also need to be flexible to address student needs. It is common in a Parallel Model to hear one teacher say to another, "We're about halfway through. Does about five more minutes sound good to you?"

Though the name "Parallel Model" implies that both groups are doing the same thing, there are times when the lesson's value is enhanced by having groups doing different things. This middle school science teacher and her special education co-teacher discuss a perfect example of the need for parallel but different activities:

> *Effective co-teachers try to synchronize before and during implementation, but also need to be flexible to student needs.*

> Mrs. Berry: "On Monday I would like to introduce students to proper technique for using a microscope. But with our class size this year, I think we'll need to have two or three students sharing each microscope."

> Mrs. Beninghof: "I can see that being a challenge for our three boys on behavior plans, as well as for Ashley and Miles in terms of attention."

> Mrs. Berry: "Unfortunately, we only have 14 working microscopes right now."

> Mrs. Beninghof: "Why don't we split the class into two groups? You can work with half the class on microscopes, while I work with the other half on reading and discussing the related chapter in the text. Then we'll switch groups halfway through the class."

> Mrs. Berry: "That sounds so much better!"

In this example, limited resources lead the teachers to choose the Parallel Model. When co-teachers choose to do different activities simultaneously, two caveats apply. First, it is important that both activities are equally engaging for students. If one group is participating in an out-of-seat, hands-on, stimulating activity and the other group is doing worksheets, students in the latter group will be very distracted. The second caveat is that the teachers should explain to students that they will all get to experience both activities. This will prevent students from feeling cheated out of a learning experience and will increase their patience while waiting.

Roles and Responsibilities

The Parallel Model is typically integrated into a Duet or Lead and Support structure. Teachers use a variety of models based on the specific learning objectives of the day and unit, and the learning needs of the students. Therefore, the Responsibilities Checklist would be dependent on the larger scope of the partners' work together. It might look like the example below or it could be more comprehensive, as in the Duet Checklist, Table 10.1.

Pros and Cons

Students who struggle mightily are likely to shut down in large groups and choose nonparticipation as a coping strategy. They quickly figure out that a teacher can't connect with every student in a class period, so it is easy to become a ghost student. Their ethereal presence can be easily missed in an overcrowded, fast-paced classroom. The Parallel Teaching Model reduces instructional group size so that students can't fade into the background. For example, in a class of thirty students with two teachers, the instructional plan might allow enough time for three students to share their personal connections to the topic. But if the class was split into two groups, the same opportunity for participation doubles. In addition, most students are more comfortable sharing their thoughts or confusion in front of a smaller group.

Consider, too, the overwhelming nature of a group of thirty students from a teacher's perspective. Caring, dedicated teachers have a desire to connect with their students, to get to know them and to make sure they are grasping the key learning concepts. But whole-group instruction can make this extremely difficult. Mrs. Travoli, a middle school language arts teacher, experienced her first Parallel Model lesson about five weeks into the first semester. Afterward, she reflected "I feel like I got to look into each student's eyes today, and

TABLE 10.1: Collaborative Teaching Responsibilities Checklist—Parallel

WHO WILL BE RESPONSIBLE FOR:	TEACHER A	TEACHER B	SHARED	COMMENTS
Identifying goals and objectives for the course?	X			
Designing individualized objectives for the targeted students?			X	
Planning instructional activities to achieve the goals?			X	
Selecting and organizing instructional materials?			X	
Teaching specific class content?			X	
Teaching study skills and learning strategies?		X		
Collecting data on student performance?			X	
Establishing and implementing grading procedures?			X	
Establishing and implementing a classroom management plan?			X	
Maintaining home contact?			X	
Modifying curriculum and materials as necessary?			X	
Designing tests, homework, and other assignments?			X	
Providing individual assistance to students?			X	
Taking care of daily routines (for example, attendance and lunch counts)?	X			
Directing paraeducators, parent volunteers, or other support personnel?	X			
Communicating to all appropriate parties regarding the targeted students?			X	

really listen to their thoughts about the passage." Rapport with her students happened because she could pull the smaller group together into a physically cohesive group and interact with each of them.

> *I feel like I got to look into each student's eyes today, and really listen to their thoughts about the passage.*

Paramount to the success of this model is the need for both teachers to be comfortable with a moderate level of classroom noise. Partners should have a conversation about ways to reduce noise distractions through careful choices of activities, physical arrangement of the space, guidelines for student voice volume, and a signaling system between teachers. For some teachers, two simultaneous activities will be too great a distraction for them. They will find it hard to concentrate on their own teaching objectives while something else is going on in the room. In these cases, the Parallel Model might need to be put on hold until a future time when teachers have developed a strong synergy.

GUIDING QUESTIONS WHEN CONSIDERING THE PARALLEL MODEL

- Are we both comfortable with a moderate amount of noise in the room?
- Are there ways we can minimize the distractions that can occur when two groups are doing similar or dissimilar activities simultaneously?
- Do we both have enough expertise in the content to use this model for initial instruction? Or is this model better used by us for application or review exercises?
- Are there times when insufficient materials might present us the perfect opportunity to use this model?

TO SUM UP

- In the Parallel Model a heterogeneous class is divided into two heterogeneous groups, with each co-teacher taking a group and providing similar instruction. This model provides for a smaller group size, yielding higher participation rates.

- Both teachers must be highly qualified in the content area if the Parallel Model will be used for content provision. If the specialist is not highly qualified, the Parallel Model can still be used for application activities.

CHAPTER 11

Adapting Model

One of the most common models in use, the Adapting Model expects one of the two teachers, usually the specialist, to make necessary accommodations and modifications so that students will be successful. Some of these adaptations might be developed in advance, but many of them are made on the spot, making this a popular model with busy teachers.

At a Glance

It is third period at Washington High School. Mr. Parache's and Mrs. Black's co-taught geometry class is taking an end-of-the-unit test. As the principal pokes her head in the door, all students appear to be doing the same thing. Given that there are several students with IEPs, whose parents are ever-vigilant about accommodations, she asks Mrs. Black to stop by her office later in the day for a chat.

After the principal expresses her concern, Mrs. Black explains:

> Mr. Parache e-mails me a copy of the test in advance. I make some format changes—things like extra space, larger font and clearer layout—and e-mail it back to him. He usually prints out copies of the same test for everyone . . . but sometimes just for the students who need the revised version. Then I audio record each test question so that students can listen to the test read aloud on iPods if they want to. The other thing we do is offer all the students in the class highlighter tape before the test. We encourage them to take a moment to look over the entire test before they begin and highlight the key directions. So when you poked

> your head in the door, we actually had three different types of accommodations in place—it just wasn't obvious. These teenagers seem much more likely to use the accommodations if we can make them subtle.

This classroom example showcases the Adapting Model at its best. Adaptations are discussed, planned for, and implemented by the co-teachers in an unobtrusive manner. Students are provided with adaptations based on need rather than on label. Everyone in this class has the opportunity to benefit from strategic adaptations.

> *Students are provided with adaptations based on need rather than on label.*

Before we delve further into this model, it will be helpful to clarify three terms that apply. *Adaptation, accommodation,* and *modification* are integral to our discussion, but are often confused and used interchangeably.

An *adaptation* is defined as the act or process of adjusting something to bring about greater success. Adaptations are used as a natural part of any teaching process and can be offered to students with and without special education labels.

An *accommodation* is defined as a change in materials or procedures that is provided to help a student fully access the general education curriculum or subject matter. An accommodation does not change the content of what is being taught nor the expectation that the student meet a performance standard applied for all students. Though this term is often used synonymously with adaptation, many educators associate it strictly with students on IEPs or 504 plans.

A *modification* is defined as a change to the general education curriculum or other material being taught that alters the standards or expectations for the student with disabilities. The student is no longer expected to be achieving at the grade level standard in a specific area of content. Modifications are usually reserved for students with more significant disabilities.

In the Adapting Model, all three processes can take place simultaneously. Teachers may agree on adaptations that are relevant to many students, with or without labels. Teachers may need to implement accommodations, based on agreements made in an IEP or

504 plan. And teachers may need to provide modifications for a student with more significant disabilities who is included in their class.

During the planning phase, co-teachers consider components of the lesson that might cause difficulty if not adapted. Common areas of concern include paper-and-pencil tests, heavy bouts of text reading, visually daunting worksheets, or socially demanding group projects. Adaptations may be discussed between the partners, or simply left as the responsibility of Teacher B to prepare.

Armed with adaptations, the instruction begins. An observer will notice Teacher A doing most of the leading, while Teacher B is providing adaptations and accommodations. Teacher A might be in the front of the room, lecturing or leading an activity, while Teacher B is wandering the room, stopping to help individual students in need of assistance. Teacher B might be seen carrying a tote, filled with strategic adaptation tools.

Strategic Adaptation Tools

- Sticky notes
- Sticky arrows
- Index cards
- Manipulatives
- Highlighters and highlighter tape
- Work masks ⊕
- Colored acetate strips ⊕
- Calculator
- Spell checker
- Correction fluid

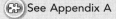See Appendix A

Ideally, someone observing over time might also notice these roles flip-flopping. Teacher A benefits enormously from having the opportunity to work one-on-one with students who are struggling. The intimacy of these interactions provides the teacher insight into a specific student's way of thinking. Is the student approaching the concept from a global or analytic perspective? Is it a specific step in the process that confuses the student, or the order of the steps? Is it a memory glitch or a comprehension problem? These opportunities also give the teacher a chance for reflection on the way he or she presented a concept—to consider if another way of teaching it might have led the student to easier acquisition.

> *The intimacy of these interactions provides the teacher insight into a specific student's way of thinking.*

Modifications are usually overseen by the specialist. These significant changes to curriculum might include finding off-grade-level texts, providing alternate assignments, using adaptive technology, or reducing homework. When modifications are provided in a co-taught class, students may voice questions or complaints. It is common to hear, "Why doesn't he have to do as much work as we do?" It will serve partners well to discuss this potential complaint in advance and agree upon a response. Co-teachers might decide to explain to students that fair treatment does not mean equal treatment, and that every student's individual needs will be considered.

During the assessment phase of teaching, Teacher B plays a vital role. As mentioned previously, adaptations to a formal assessment usually happen before it has been distributed. Borrowing from the concept of universal design, teachers should attempt to design a test that will not need to be adapted! Effective test design principles include those shown in Exhibit 11.1.

There are instances when a student may need specific accommodations that have been agreed to in his IEP. These might include having tests read aloud, using a scribe, or repeating test directions. In the past, these types of accommodations would have resulted in an instant assumption that the student would need to leave the room. In co-teaching, every attempt is made to keep the student in the room during testing. Why? Thanks to memory researchers, educators now know that learning environments are filled with invisible information that can aid student recall. For example, a student being tested on Newton's first law of motion may form a mental picture of the balloon experiment done in class . . . if they are taking the test in the same classroom where the experiment occurred. Cues in the environment will lead the brain to fire up the neural pathways used in the original learning experience.

EXHIBIT 11.1: Test Design and Adaptation

Points to consider when designing matching items:

- Same number of items in each column
- Longer items in the left column, shorter in the right
- All items on one page
- Not more than ten items

Points to consider when designing sentence completion items:

- Use cues, such as blanks or first letters
- Use simple sentences
- Offer a word bank

Points to consider when designing true/false items

- Not more than ten items
- Avoid negative sentences
- Avoid double negatives in a sentence
- Use simple sentences
- Avoid tricky words such as "always"

Points to consider when designing essays and short answer items:

- Allow student to sketch a plan
- Specify the number of examples, points required
- Avoid complex sentences
- Offer choice of paper

Points to consider when designing multiple choice items:

- List items vertically
- No more than four choices
- Avoid combination answers, such as "all of the above"
- Use simple sentences

Points to consider when designing any test:

- Use Arial font
- Use 14 point
- Use a mixture of upper and lower case letters

On the rare occasion when a student's individual challenges require that he be removed to an alternative testing environment, the specialist will typically leave the room with him. This exodus should be as unobtrusive as possible to minimize embarrassment for the student. At the secondary level, teachers often arrange in advance for the student to go directly to the alternative space, rather than having to exit class after it has begun.

Roles and Responsibilities

The role of Teacher B is very limited in the Adapting Model, as detailed in Table 11.1, causing the benefits of this co-teaching model to also be very limited. While there are some schools that utilize just this model and claim to be co-teaching, they are doing so in a very minimalist fashion. Teacher B is operating more like a paraeducator than a highly trained professional, and even in that role is underutilized. However, if the co-teachers blend this model with several others, then the specialist is truly a partner in the teaching process and all students benefit.

Pros and Cons

Three small but distinct advantages accompany the Adapting Model. First, this model is time efficient, if used as a stand-alone model. The co-teachers need very little common planning time. Instead, the general educator can provide a copy of the lesson plan by e-mail or mailbox, and the specialist can choose appropriate adaptations. The specialist can arrive in the room armed with her toolbox and wander around the room to support specific students. Of course, this lack of co-planning has disadvantages, as will be discussed below.

The second advantage is that it encourages one of the two teachers to focus specifically on individualizing instruction for targeted students. Usually, targeted students have struggled with whole-group, one-size-fits-all instruction and have demonstrated a

TABLE 11.1: Collaborative Teaching Responsibilities Checklist—Adapting

WHO WILL BE RESPONSIBLE FOR:	TEACHER A	TEACHER B	SHARED	COMMENTS
Identifying goals and objectives for the course?	X			
Designing individualized objectives for the targeted students?			X	
Planning instructional activities to achieve the goals?	X			
Selecting and organizing instructional materials?			X	Teacher B only manages adapted materials
Teaching specific class content?	X			
Teaching study skills and learning strategies?	X			
Collecting data on student performance?			X	Teacher B only on targeted students
Establishing and implementing grading procedures?	X			
Establishing and implementing a classroom management plan?	X			
Maintaining home contact?			X	Usually divided rather than collaborative
Modifying curriculum and materials as necessary?		X		
Designing tests, homework, and other assignments?			X	
Providing individual assistance to students?		X		
Taking care of daily routines (for example, attendance and lunch counts)?	X			
Directing paraeducators, parent volunteers, or other support personnel?	X			
Communicating to all appropriate parties regarding the targeted students?			X	Usually divided rather than collaborative

clear need for something different. In the Adapting Model, Teacher B has the mandate to present these students with adaptations designed to meet their unique needs.

Closely linked to these first two benefits, the third advantage to the Adapting Model is that it delineates clear responsibility to one of the partners for ensuring that IEP or 504 Plan commitments are kept. In the high-energy, co-taught classroom, it is easy to lose sight of specific legal agreements. Collaborative partners are busy with co-managing many facets of the instructional process, and specific accommodations can be overlooked. The Adapting Model strives to avoid this problem by not
only clarifying responsibility for these, but also highlighting this responsibility.

Two major concerns jump immediately to mind when the Adapting Model is used as a stand-alone. First, as alluded to earlier, the lack of co-planning can lead to weak interventions. If Teacher B doesn't fully understand the nature of the lesson, adaptations may miss the mark or end up being trivial. The adaptations seem like a band-aid, rather than a healthy, preventative measure. It is just not possible for Teacher B to provide high-quality adaptations if she is not involved in ongoing conversation with Teacher A.

The second major concern is that Teacher B is underutilized in the Adapting Model. Though her skills in providing accommodations and modifications will be applied to individual students, any other teaching skills she has will go untapped. This is especially true in the case of a highly trained professional specialist. This model puts her in a role that could easily be assumed by someone with fewer qualifications (and lower on the pay scale.)

With these concerns in mind, the question arises "Should we use the Adapting Model at all?" The answer is "Yes!"—in conjunction with other models to form a more comprehensive approach to collaboration.

GUIDING QUESTIONS WHEN CONSIDERING
THE ADAPTING MODEL

- How can we communicate thoroughly enough about the lesson plan to ensure that the adaptations are relevant and effective?
- How will we respond to student complaints about different or reduced assignments?
- Are there obvious times when Teacher A and B roles can be swapped?
- Will we blend this model with other models to ensure that Teacher B's expertise is fully utilized?

TO SUM UP

- In the most common approach to the Adapting Model, the specialist provides small changes to instruction and assessment that make learning more accessible for targeted students. This can be planned for in advance or developed on the spot. Less common, but still valuable, is when the classroom teacher offers the adaptations to students who need them.
- Although this model is an important asset to a co-taught class, it is best when paired with other models so that the skills of the specialist are more fully utilized.

CHAPTER 12

Complementary Skills Model

"Last but not least" is a common phrase that applies well to the
Complementary Skills Model. This model is essential to co-teaching between
a general educator and a specialist because it sets a clear expectation that
specialized instruction will occur in the mainstream setting.

At a Glance

Mrs. Lindsey scans the IEP objectives for the students in her co-taught history class. She notices that four of the students have objectives that are similar—"The student will be able to identify main idea and supporting details in a nonfiction passage. . . . " By high school, most general education teachers assume that students have these skills and do not teach it in a direct manner. Mrs. Lindsey decides to approach her co-teacher, Mr. Kalotay, with the idea of providing a mini-lesson on main idea, embedded into the content of the class.

Mr. Kalotay expresses his concern. "I feel like we are starting to get behind on our pacing guide. I am not sure I can justify adding this when it will only benefit a few of the students."

Mrs. Lindsey carefully counters, "When we analyzed the tests from our last unit, we felt that many of the students were struggling with seeing the main concepts and overriding themes. I think we will find that students other than those with IEPs will benefit from this. And I can try to think of a way to ramp it up for some of our higher level thinkers." The co-teachers agree to weave this instruction into the text-based lessons, using just a few minutes in each lesson and adding a component to the homework assignments. Their plan takes shape as shown in Table 12.1.

TABLE 12.1: Complementary Skills Lesson Plan

Objective: Students will be able to identify main idea, supporting detail, and theme (optional) in the U.S. Government text, Branches of Government Unit	
PERSON RESPONSIBLE: TEACHER A	**PERSON RESPONSIBLE: TEACHER B**
PROCEDURE	PROCEDURE
• Temple Strategy • Start class with photo of a Greek temple • Discuss temple as a metaphor—columns as supporting details, roof as main idea, and cloud overhead as theme • Provide students with temple graphic organizer to complete for homework • After metaphor has been introduced, begin reading text pp. 129–132 • Stop occasionally to match components of text to pieces of temple	• Add lecture notes to enhance text reading • Challenge students to think of the "theme"—the universal concept involved • Remainder of unit—ask students to draw a temple in their notes and complete it for each chunk of new content

See Appendix A

The focus of the Complementary Skills Model is on the skills students need to access the general education curriculum that aren't typically part of the standard curriculum. These skills complement the traditional instruction. In Colorado, these kinds of skills are called *access skills* or *expanded standards* because without them it will be difficult, if not impossible, for a student to access the standards. Primary grades teachers often weave these skills into lessons and incidental learning opportunities. Some students will need direct instruction on these skills well into their secondary years.

The Complementary Skills Model expands as the specialist gets to know the targeted students and perceives gaps between their current skill level and the expectations for the class. This usually occurs after the school year has begun, unless the specialist has in-depth prior knowledge about the students. As the partners implement their co-teaching plan, they become aware of some missing complementary skills. Together they decide if these skills are things that the students can absorb through modeling and informal

TABLE 12.2: Colorado Department of Education, Expanded Standards

COMMUNICATION AND BASIC LANGUAGE	SELF-ADVOCACY/SELF-DETERMINATION
Attending Listening Interpreting meaning Responding to others Expressing self Gaining/maintaining attention Following and giving directions Consistently attaching meaning to symbol Acknowledging and honoring other's statements of needs, wants and feeling Using alternative communication methods Other:	Asking for and/or accepting peer support Assessing situations for equal access and asking for adjustments when appropriate Expressing physical needs Expressing personal preferences and choices Expressing simple feeling states Expressing other feeling states Expressing understanding of difference Describing personal learning limitations Negotiating adjustments Evaluating effectiveness of a variety of learning strategies and making adjustments as needed Developing and maintaining a supportive network Acting independently based on knowledge of personal needs and preferences Advocating for others as well as issues and ideas Using self-regulation techniques Engaging in sustained participation Applying conflict management techniques Dealing with change Other:
DECISION MAKING AND PROBLEM SOLVING	**PHYSICAL**
Using conflict resolution Self-initiating activities, tasks, assignments, etc. Setting goals to plan for action Using discretionary time in appropriate ways Self-monitoring behavior, time Advocating for self and needs Persuading others Indicating understanding of cause/effect Other:	Maintaining acceptable personal appearance Managing physical/medical needs Mobility Manipulating materials and equipment Other:
INTER/INTRAPERSONAL	**TECHNOLOGY**
Demonstrating socially acceptable behaviors Demonstrating appropriate behavior to the group Cooperatively working with others in group situation Demonstrating social amenities Gaining/maintaining interest/leisure skills Other:	Demonstrating computer literacy Selecting technology appropriate to the situation Applying technology Using keyboard skills Using input devices (mouse) Accessing computer system Selecting and using appropriate software Using technology information Other:

exposure, or if they need to adjust their lesson plans to include targeted instruction.

If the partners determine the need for purposefully constructed instruction for complementary skills, it is usually the role of the specialist to craft this component of the lesson. This may occur through a warm-up activity, a five-minute mini-lesson, a closure activity, or it can be embedded throughout an entire period. Keep in mind that a student who is missing an age-appropriate complementary skill has clearly had difficulty picking up this skill through one-shot lessons or subtle exposure. To achieve success, the partners will most likely have to return to this skill multiple times throughout the semester. The specialist can speed up the acquisition process by looking for ways to build bridges across differing contexts.

Most students in a co-taught class will not be assessed on their complementary skills. Targeted students might be. If the targeted student has an IEP which identifies a complementary skill as an objective, progress monitoring will need to occur. Likewise, if the school or district has some other process in place for identifying individual objectives beyond the standards, the teachers may need to collect data on complementary skills.

Roles and Responsibilities

Many of the models are designed in such a way that the roles of Teacher A and Teacher B can be easily swapped. The Complementary Skills Model is different. Complementary skills are often identified as objectives on a special education IEP and go beyond the realm of the typical curriculum content. They may require "specially designed instruction"—a professional skill set for which special education teachers and other specialists receive training and certification. Because of their qualifications, specialists will adopt the role of Teacher B in almost all circumstances. This means that they will accept the primary responsibility for designing, implementing, and assessing the complementary skill aspect of the co-taught class. However, conversations between partners can spark insights for the specialist that might have remained hidden. Collaboration will improve the process!

TABLE 12.3: Collaborative Teaching Responsibilities Checklist—Complementary Skills

WHO WILL BE RESPONSIBLE FOR:	TEACHER A	TEACHER B	SHARED	COMMENTS
Identifying goals and objectives for the course?	X			
Designing individualized objectives for the targeted students?		X		
Planning instructional activities to achieve the goals?	X	X		A: Content B: Complementary Skills
Selecting and organizing instructional materials?			X	
Teaching specific class content?	X			
Teaching study skills and learning strategies?		X		
Collecting data on student performance?			X	Teacher B: Data on Complementary Skills
Establishing and implementing grading procedures?			X	
Establishing and implementing a classroom management plan?			X	
Maintaining home contact?			X	
Modifying curriculum and materials as necessary?		X		
Designing tests, homework, and other assignments?			X	
Providing individual assistance to students?		X		
Taking care of daily routines (for example, attendance and lunch counts)?	X			
Directing paraeducators, parent volunteers, or other support personnel?	X			
Communicating to all appropriate parties regarding the targeted students?			X	Usually divided rather than collaborative

Pros and Cons

The primary reason for the boom in co-teaching has been inclusive education. Educators, parents, and policymakers recognized the advantages of participation in general education classrooms—access to curriculum, content experts, role models, and high expectations. However, students with unique needs also need instruction from professionals uniquely qualified to address their needs. The No Child Left Behind Act of 2001 (NCLB) supported this recognition by requiring that students in special education have access to teachers who are highly qualified in their domain. The most efficient and effective way to accomplish this is through co-teaching between a general education teacher and a specialist.

The Complementary Skills Model is the only model whose sole purpose is to focus on access skills that students are missing. Its advantage is that it clearly expects specially designed instruction to take place in the general education classroom. By using this model, there is no chance that those individual skills will be ignored or overlooked by busy teachers. Instead, the specialist pays particular attention to ways to address those skills within the classroom context.

A perceived disadvantage of this model is that the pacing of the class will slow down. This is a valid concern for teachers who operate under the extreme pressure of covering certain content in a given time frame. It seems as if adding a focus on complementary skills is one more thing to fit into a very full day. Partners will want to find creative ways to embed complementary skills into their lesson plans so that any additional time required is not significant. Partners will also want to monitor their pacing carefully—checking with other teachers to ensure that a common pace is being maintained.

> *Partners will want to find creative ways to embed complementary skills into their lesson plans so that any additional time required is not significant.*

GUIDING QUESTIONS WHEN CONSIDERING THE COMPLEMENTARY SKILLS MODEL

- How many of our students have the need for complementary skills instruction? Do those skill needs easily group into common categories?
- Are there certain days, times, or components of the curriculum into which it will be easiest to embed complementary skills?
- Can we identify a system for checking the pacing of our class?
- Will we use just this model, or can we blend it with others to be even more effective?

TO SUM UP

- In the Complementary Skills Model, Teacher B pays special attention to the learning skills students need to access the general curriculum. Once identified, these skills are addressed through mini-lessons or woven into whole group instruction.
- The Complementary Skills Model provides a clear path for specialists to ensure they are addressing IEP objectives, or other student-specific mandates, without isolating the students to do so.

DISCUSSION QUESTIONS FOR PART TWO

- Which of the co-teaching models require the least amount of co-planning time? The most? How does collaboration time affect instructional quality?

- Which models place an emphasis on differentiated instruction? How do they compare in their approach to differentiation?

- For a specialist who lacks confidence in the curriculum content, which model might serve as a good entry point for co-teaching?

- What are some steps a co-teacher can take to ensure that he or she is not underutilized in the classroom?

- Which models have the potential for isolating or embarrassing targeted students? What can be done to avoid that outcome?

- What advice would you give someone who is trying to choose a model for his or her co-teaching partnership?

- Which models do you think students will find most appealing? Why?

PART THREE

CREATING A UNIQUE DESIGN FOR WORKING TOGETHER

CHAPTER 13

Co-Teaching with a Technology Specialist

Mrs. Goldman's third-grade classroom is quiet with anticipation. Her twenty-seven students have their desktops cleared, eyes on the doorway, as Mrs. Blair enters, wheeling a technology cart loaded with thirty laptops. The students know what to do. The laptops are efficiently distributed and students power up while Mrs. Blair connects to a multimedia projector for demonstration purposes. Today's lesson is a continuation of a four-day project on how to create online multimedia posters that Mrs. Blair has been co-teaching with each of the third-grade teachers.

Mrs. Goldman asks "Does everyone have a copy of their Solar System contract on their desk?" The students have developed individual contracts, based on their experience, that commit them to learning new technology skills in this project. Mrs. Goldman reminds them of content requirements for their multimedia posters and draws their attention to a chart posted on the wall that includes key information.

Almost like a tennis match, the ball goes back to Mrs. Blair's court. She models the process for logging in to the specific website, reminds students of major tools, and demonstrates one of the more tricky steps. Before letting students move ahead on their own, Mrs. Goldman queries, "Do you need to be patient?" and then both teachers roam the room offering individual support. As puzzled children begin to raise their hands for help, Mrs. Blair kindly reminds them, "If you can't remember how to import, you need to ask three friends before me."

Co-teaching with technology specialists is on the rise. In Douglas County School District, just south of Denver, Colorado, approximately one-fourth of the technology teachers are currently co-teaching, with more embracing the concept each year. Why the rapid increase in interest? Students entering schools are digital natives, having been raised in a culture rife with technology. Access to computers in their homes, libraries, and pockets has led to a shift in how they spend their free time, and a shift in their expectations. Don Tapscott, author and entrepreneur, catalogues these changes in his book, *Grown Up Digital*. He describes these "Net Geners" as "active initiators, collaborators, organizers, readers, writers, authenticators and strategists. They do not just observe; they participate. They inquire, discuss, argue, play, shop, critique, investigate, ridicule, fantasize, seek and inform" (2009, 21). And they do all of this with and through technology that is second nature to them.

Teachers, on the other hand, are primarily digital immigrants, encountering technology as if it is a second language to learn. Busy with day-to-day teaching demands, many teachers are reluctant to study the language and applications of technology, in addition to keeping up with emerging research in their content areas. A gap exists between student needs and teacher skills. Co-teaching bridges this gap. The technology specialist has current expertise with which to keep students engaged and moving forward, while at the same time modeling for the general educator. Through gradual release, this expertise becomes part of the classroom teacher's repertoire.

> *The technology specialist has current expertise with which to keep students engaged and moving forward, while at the same time modeling for the general educator.*

Best Models

The Complementary Skills Model is the approach used most often by general education/technology specialist teams. This model expects both partners to have a unique instructional expertise that should be woven together to form an integrated lesson, but doesn't expect the specialist to fully share other responsibilities, such as classroom and materials management. The Complementary Skills Model also includes a more realistic expectation regarding co-planning. The specialist is not a full participant in planning every unit and lesson, but is involved in planning the lessons through which they will infuse their particular specialty.

Though this model provides the underlying structure for their work together, these co-teachers are also likely to use the Speak and Add Model throughout the lesson. If the specialist directs the students using "computer-speak" and the classroom teacher notices that some don't understand, she might ask the technology teacher to restate in more familiar language. Or perhaps the classroom teacher is describing some of the elements shown on a Word document and the specialist will use the highlight function to focus students visually. These interactions are natural and fluent, not written into the lesson plan.

Challenges

Co-planning can be a challenge for all teams, but provides unique problems when working with a technology specialist. It is very common for specialists to develop their schedules by periods of the day, with the intent of having a consistent schedule. For example, a speech/language therapist might arrange to co-teach in a fifth-grade classroom every Wednesday during a forty-five-minute book club activity. Technology specialists need to arrange their schedules very differently for effective co-teaching. Many of the technology skills we want students to learn need to be taught and practiced for several consecutive days to be meaningful. Let's say that the objective is for students to learn how to use a Web 2.0 poster application, incorporating a variety of media and links, to show their knowledge about the solar system. Working on this once a week for more than a month is not going to lead to retention. Instead, an intense infusion of technology practice over the course of several consecutive days will be more effective.

Now consider the fact that every class in a building will need technology instruction, and yet the building probably only has one technology specialist. Scheduling has just become much more complicated. The specialist must build a schedule that allows her to co-teach with every teacher in the building so that she can access

> *Technology specialists need to arrange their schedules very differently for effective co-teaching.*

every child. Project-based scheduling is the solution. In project-based scheduling the principal works with the faculty to set a goal of five or six technology infusions or projects per year for each teacher. The specialist meets with each grade level or department to look at their plan for the quarter or semester. Together they identify the units and projects that might lend themselves to technology infusion, along with tentative time lines. The specialist builds her schedule by fitting in as many of the opportunities as possible, while balancing her time among all the teachers. Table 13.1 illustrates an example of project-based scheduling.

TABLE 13.1: Technology Co-Teaching Schedule

OCTOBER 17	OCTOBER 18	OCTOBER 19	OCTOBER 20	OCTOBER 21
9:25–10:05 6A Economics Unit	9:25–10:05 6A Economics Unit	9:25–10:05 6A Economics Unit	9:25–10:05 6A Economics Unit	9:25–10:05 6A Economics Unit
10:10–11:00 3rd grade planning meeting	10:10–10:30 6B Google Earth Latin America	10:10–11:00 5th grade planning meeting	10:10–10:30 6C Google Earth Latin America	10:10–11:00 Tech repairs
	10:30–11:00 KB Tumblebooks		10:30–11:00 KA Tumblebooks	
11:00–11:45 KC Tumblebooks	11:00–11:45 3A Solar System Glogster	11:00–11:45 3A Solar System Glogster	11:00–11:45 3A Solar System Glogster	11:00–11:45 3A Solar System Glogster
11:45–12:15 Tech repairs				
1:00–1:50 2B Kidpix Autobiography Unit	1:00–1:50 2B Kidpix Autobiography Unit	1:00–1:50 2B Kidpix Autobiography Unit	1:00–1:50 2B Typing Pal Autobiography Unit	1:00–1:502B Typing Pal Autobiography Unit
1:50–2:30 5C Mini Society Ads	1:50–2:30 5C Mini Society Ads	1:50–2:30 5C Mini Society Ads, iPhoto	1:50–2:30 5C Mini Society Ads, iPhoto	1:50–2:30 5C Mini Society Ads, video links
2:30–3:15 1A Math Fact Families, IWB	2:30–3:15 1A Math Fact Families, IWB	2:30–3:15 4B xtranormal.com	2:30–3:15 4B xtranormal.com	2:30–3:15 4B xtranormal.com

TABLE 13.1: Technology Co-Teaching Schedule—cont'd

OCTOBER 24	OCTOBER 25	OCTOBER 26	OCTOBER 27	OCTOBER 28
9:25–10:05 6A Economics Unit	9:25–10:05 6 A Economics Unit	9:25–10:05 6A Economics Unit	9:25–10:05 6A Economics Unit	9:25–10:05 6A Economics Unit
10:10–11:00 4A Newsletter podcasts	10:10–11:00 4A Newsletter podcasts	10:10–11:00 4A Newsletter podcasts	10:10–11:00 4A Newsletter podcasts	10:10–11:00 4A Newsletter podcasts
11:00–11:45 5A Bacteria Prezis	11:00–11:45 5A Bacteria Prezis	11:00–11:45 5A Bacteria Prezis	11:00–11:45 1C Flash Cards online	11:00–11:45 1C Flash Cards online
1:00–1:50 2B Kidpix Autobiography Unit	1:00–1:50 2B Kidpix Autobiography Unit	1:00–1:50 2B Kidpix Autobiography Unit	1:00–1:40 1st grade planning meeting	1:00–1:50 Tech repairs
1:50–2:30 5C Mini Society Ads final	1:50–2:30 1C Timeliner	1:50–2:30 1C Timeliner	1:50–2:30 1C Timeliner	1:50–2:30 1C Timeliner
2:30–3:15 1B Math Fact Families, IWB	2:30–3:15 1B Math Fact Families, IWB	2:30- 3:15 4B xtranormal.com	2:30–3:15 4B xtranormal.com	2:30–3:15 4B xtranormal.com

An additional challenge is caused by project-based scheduling. Because the specialist works in the classroom on an irregular basis, the potential is present for teachers to forget their scheduled time. When classroom teachers are unprepared due to oversight, the specialist's time is underutilized. Debbie Blair voiced this frustration: "Once in awhile I arrive at a class to find that the teacher has forgotten I am coming. Even if she can drop everything, it may not work because there might have been a certain amount of content preparation that the students needed to accomplish before I arrived" (personal communication, 2010). An effective communication strategy must be developed to help everyone remember their scheduled commitments.

Essential for Success

In many elementary and middle schools, technology is treated like a "special." The principal builds technology into the master schedule in a way similar to art, music, library, and physical education, so that it provides a "free" planning period. For co-teaching with a technology specialist to be successful, the principal must change this practice so that the classroom teacher is available and expected to participate in the technology-infused lesson. This may require creative planning and new additions to the specials rotation.

At Prairie Crossing Elementary School in Parker, Colorado, Principal Tom McDowell approached his School Advisory Committee to garner their support for co-teaching technology. After a brief presentation and discussion, parents and teachers enthusiastically embraced the idea. With student-based budgeting, McDowell and his committee had the freedom to decide how to structure the staffing in his building to accomplish their goals. They decided to remove the technology specialist from the specials rotation. Though McDowell continues to provide his teachers with a daily planning period, he now does so with art, music, physical education, library, and Spanish. McDowell believes that "co-teaching is the most effective form of professional development we have. If you truly want technology to not be ancillary to the curriculum, then co-teaching should be required" (personal communication, 2010). His strong belief in the value of co-taught technology is creating a school where faculty and students are developing essential twenty-first-century skills.

TO SUM UP

- Co-teaching with a technology specialist is on the rise as educators recognize the benefit of integrating technology into all areas of instruction. Usually technology specialists employ the Complementary Skills and Speak and Add Models while they co-teach.

- Creative scheduling will ensure the most comprehensive use of the technology specialist's expertise and provide students with enough time to acquire the new skills.

DISCUSSION QUESTIONS

- What factors are causing an increase in co-teaching with technology specialists?

- Why is scheduling for co-teaching with a technology specialist more difficult than with other specialists? What are some ideas for meeting the challenges?

- Which co-teaching models do you feel would be most effective? Why?

CHAPTER 14

Co-Teaching with a Special Education Teacher

From: Lora.Hamilton@suburbanschool.org

To: Anne.Beninghof@suburbanschool.org

CC: Barb.Kalisch@suburbanschool.org; Grace.Helgeson@suburbanschool.org; Alicia.Osborn@suburbanschool.org

Re: Thursday

Hi Anne,

We just finished planning and identified a problem area. With CSAP coming up, we would like to see if you have any strategies that would help the kids focus in on multi-step directions. These strategies need to be easy to use and applicable to a standardized testing environment. (In other words, no standing on chairs, etc. . . . ☺)

L

From: Anne.Beninghof@suburbanschool.org

To: Lora.Hamilton@suburbanschool.org

CC: Barb.Kalisch@suburbanschool.org; Grace.Helgeson@suburbanschool.org; Alicia.Osborn@suburbanschool.org

Re: Thursday

Lora,

Got it. Still engaging, but no standing on chairs! Please e-mail me a few examples of the types of questions or question formats that you are most concerned about or post them to your grade level wiki. I'll also find a few that I think students struggle with, and think of a way to integrate a strategy into the content that is planned for Thursday.

A

From: Anne.Beninghof@suburbanschool.org

To: Lora.Hammil@suburbanschool.org

CC: Barb.Kalisch@suburbanschool.org; Grace.Helgeson@suburbanschool.org

Alicia.Osborn@suburbanschool.org

Re: Thursday

Lora, Barb, Grace and Alicia:

Here's the plan for Thursday. I'll take the lead and you can jump in with content clarifications, etc. I am attaching an activity page for you to copy that has similar problems to the following.

1. Draw a triangle. Put a circle inside it. Draw a square around the circle.
2. Write the word "fun" on your paper. Underline it three times.
3. Stand up and hop on one foot three times. Laugh. Then sit down again.
4. Think about someone special in your life. Write their name on your paper and three words that describe them.

We can take turns modeling for students how to put a check boxed next to each part of a multi-step direction. We'll have students discuss how many boxes are called for and where they should go. As they do the task, they check off the box. My plan is to bring in a large box and place it next to the projector. When a student comes up to demonstrate they will stand in the box to add a visual/kinesthetic emphasis.

A

Special education teachers have a kaleidoscope, or lens, that is different from that of their general education counterparts. They have the ability to look at specific tasks, break them down into their smallest components, diagnose difficulties, and brainstorm unique instructional solutions. This ability is ripe for replication in inclusive classrooms. Co-teaching is the instrument for sharing this skill set so that all class members benefit.

Co-teaching between special education and general education teachers has been occurring in some schools for many years. Forward thinkers saw the need for students with disabilities to have access to general education curriculum *and* access to an educator with training in specially designed instruction. They also saw the social benefits of inclusion for students with and without disabilities. But the advent of the No Child Left Behind Act of 2001 (NCLB) increased the urgency of adoption. This act, like the reauthorization of the Individuals with Disabilities Education Act (IDEA), set requirements for high standards and performance for all students. The mandate that students have access to general education curriculum and highly qualified teachers has forced special education departments to reevaluate their service delivery models. Especially at the secondary level, it is difficult to find teachers who have certifications in special education and one or more content areas—teachers who meet the "highly qualified" standard in both general and special education. Districts are moving to co-teaching as the solution.

Best Models

Strong special education/general education partnerships blend all of the models of co-teaching together to serve students. The Duet Model, with comprehensive collaboration throughout all phases of instruction, makes the most sense. With this model, specially designed instruction is built into the unit plans from the very beginning, rather than as an add-on. However, most special education teachers need to support students distributed among several classrooms and do not have the time necessary to implement the Duet Model. It is typical for special education teachers to be assigned to co-teach with three to five general education teachers, often in different content areas. In these cases, the Duet Model is unrealistic.

The Skill Groups Model lends itself well to special and general education co-teaching. In this model, the teachers plan lessons that incorporate multiple instructional levels (Beninghof, 2008; Tomlinson, 1999). At times this might involve breaking students into skill-based small groups. At other times, this might involve planning a whole group lesson that is imbedded with challenges and supports for multiple learning levels. This model ensures that students with disabilities are provided with learning tasks that are not too frustrating, while still moving them forward in the general education curriculum. Ideally, the two teachers will sit together to plan every detail of the lesson, but the planning can also be done more efficiently by dividing responsibilities. Once this division is clear, they can each plan specific details on their own.

The Complementary Skills Model is also a good match for special education co-teaching. In this model, the expectation is very clear that specially designed instruction will take place within the general education classroom. IEP objectives are reviewed weekly to guarantee that instruction addresses the commitment made to students and parents. Co-teaching partners continually check that the strategies used in the classroom are moving students toward accomplishing their goals. For example, an IEP objective for one student might state, "The student will be able to follow three-step, printed directions (when content skills are already acquired) with 90% accuracy." Though this objective is highly individualized, it is very likely that other students in the class have similar IEP objectives. It is also highly likely that there are several students in the class who do not have a special education label but still have difficulty following multistep directions. The special education teacher will use her expertise to develop a related strategy that can be infused into the general education content so that all students will benefit.

The Speak and Add Model will be frequently evident in a special education/general education co-taught class. The special educator will be listening for opportunities to clarify and restate information that

> " *Co-teaching partners continually check that the strategies used in the classroom are moving students toward accomplishing their goals.* "

may be presented at a higher complexity level than some students can follow. Whenever appropriate, a special educator might support the teacher's lecture with graphic organizers, relevant pictures, mnemonics, and other simple nonlinguistic representations. Sometimes these are planned in advance, but much of the time specialists are tapping into their expertise on the spot and jumping in with the supportive device.

Because so many students in special education respond well to tactile and kinesthetic instruction (Carbo, 2009; Hodgin and Wooliscraft, 1997) the Learning Style Model lends itself well to this type of co-taught class. In addition, many researchers advocate multimodality instruction as beneficial for all students (Willis, 2008; Ratey, 2008; Haynes, 2007; Gurian, 2005). Pre-service training for special educators usually has a strong focus on hands-on instructional strategies. With this training and expertise, the specialist can be continuously scanning the curriculum plan for opportunities to weave in tactile and kinesthetic experiences.

Tenth graders in Mr. Simon's English class were reading the autobiography *Night* by Elie Wiesel, concurrent with the History Department's unit on World War II and the Holocaust. The lesson planning form that he and his special education co-teacher use includes prompts that remind them of essential lesson elements for their particular students (See Exhibit 14.1.) With another class, the prompts might differ depending on the unique needs of the students. During their quick planning session, Mrs. Brannick, the special education teacher, offered ideas aimed at meeting the IEP objectives and making the content accessible to struggling students.

EXHIBIT 14.1: Co-Teaching English with a Special Education Teacher

Lesson Plan for: *English 10 "Night" by Elie Wiesel*

Instructional Objective(s): Students will identify examples of characterization; will employ strategies to extend writing

Does the lesson address the following elements?

- ☐ Attention Grabbing/Maintaining
- ☐ Organization Skills
- ☐ Retention
- ☐ Auditory/Visual Perception
- ☐ Specific 504 accommodations

- ☐ Participation
- ☐ Varied groupings
- ☐ Connections
- ☐ Multimodality
- ☐ Specific IEP objectives

Process

Attention Grabber: Mrs. A to moan loudly and continually in corner of room as if in pain while Mr. S. ignores. After a minute or so, talk with students about their reactions, and make connections to the moaning, screaming character in Night.

Review vocabulary: characterization, flat and round, etc., on board, color coded.

Use Deal or No Deal Strategy ✹ to practice vocabulary in contexts. Whole group.

Character Layers Activity: ✹ Mrs. A will model by describing various character traits (physical, behavioral, psychological) of Mr. S. to whole group. Students will work in pairs. Mrs. A. will distribute markers and transparency strips while Mr. S assigns one of four characters:

Madame Schacter
Elie Wiesel
Elie's father
Moishe the Beadle

Writing Prompt: Show prompt on screen and highlight key words during read through. Give students 45 seconds to illustrate their reaction, then 10 minutes to write in journal. Both teachers wander and offer support.

✹ See Appendix A

Challenges

A student receiving special education services is guaranteed, by law, an individualized education program. In a co-taught classroom with thirty students, there might be as many as ten students with individualized programs. The challenge co-teachers face is to find creative ways to address student's individual needs within the general education context, without slowing down the pacing, or embarrassing certain students. Co-teachers share the obligation to try to accomplish the IEP objectives relevant to the class, *and* the obligation to bring all students to mastery of the course objectives. The difficulty lies in managing both.

For example, picture a student who has decoding and fluency skills on a fifth-grade level, but is in an eighth-grade language arts class. There are three other students like him. Another student in the class has IEP objectives geared toward writing conventions. Two others have accommodations for attention deficits, one has Asperger's syndrome. The co-teachers of this class often design flexible lessons that allow for individual readiness levels and student choice. But these teachers also believe there is benefit in activities that involve all students. So they must be able to create whole-group strategies that effectively address multiple levels while still matching the pace of similar, solo-taught classes. Success will require your *best teachers*. Teachers who are weak, exhibit control issues, are poor communicators, and lack creativity are not good candidates for the challenges of co-teaching a class with a high percentage of struggling students.

Essential for Success

Both teachers must view all students as "ours" rather than "yours" and "mine." Evidence for this commitment can be subtle and not so subtle:

- Both teachers' names on the board.
- Teachers using phrases such as "When we grade your papers . . ." or "What we expect . . ."

- Letters home that are signed by both teachers.

- Report cards that include both teachers' names.

If a duality or separation exists between the teachers or students because of a special education label, success will be limited. Administrators should recruit teachers who fully embrace an inclusive philosophy.

> *Administrators should recruit teachers who fully embrace an inclusive philosophy.*

Class composition must be balanced. When a special educator is assigned to co-teach a class, it is tempting for administrators to place all of the needy students in that class, whether or not they have a disability label. Before anyone realizes it, the class can become filled with struggling students. Without mixed-ability grouping, the class may not have appropriate role models for academic or behavioral success. But if an administrator evenly divides the students with disabilities across all classrooms, the special education teacher will be spread too thin to be able to co-teach. Some amount of "loading" classrooms is likely to be necessary. Inclusive classrooms that work best will have no more than 30 percent of the students with IEPs, and the remaining 70 percent will include a blend of on- and above-grade-level students. In some regions of the country, state education departments are instituting regulations aimed at maintaining a similar balance in the classroom.

Because co-teaching requires co-planning, a special educator will not be able to co-teach with more than four teachers. If she is assigned to more than four classes, she will, of necessity, be providing in-class support rather than co-teaching. Success will also be boosted if the special education teacher's class assignments are narrowed by grade level or content. For example, an elementary specialist might co-teach in just first and second grade, whereas a high school specialist might co-teach in just English courses. Table 14.1 shows two possible schedules for a special education teacher.

TABLE 14.1: Special Education Co-Teaching Schedules

EXAMPLE ONE					
	M	T	W	TH	F
7:55- 8:50	Indirect Support	Indirect Support	Indirect Support	Indirect Support	Indirect Support
8:55—9:45	Co-Teach	Co-Teach	Co-Teach	Co-Teach	Co-Teach
9:50–10:30	Prep	Prep	Prep	Prep	Prep
10:35—11: 25	Co-Teach	Co-Teach	Co-Teach	Co-Teach	Co-Teach
11:30—12:05	Lunch	Lunch	Lunch	Lunch	Lunch
12:15—1:05	Co-Teach	Co-Teach	Co-Teach	Co-Teach	Co-Teach
1:10–2:00	Co-Teach	Co-Teach	Co-Teach	Co-Teach	Co-Teach
2:05–2:55	Learning Center	Learning Center	Learning Center	Learning Center	Learning Center

EXAMPLE TWO					
	M	T	W	TH	F
7:55–8:50	Learning Center	Learning Center	Learning Center	Indirect Support	Learning Center
8:55–9:45	Co-Teach	Co-Teach	Co-Teach	Indirect Support	Co-Teach
9:50–10:30	Prep	Prep	Prep	Prep	Prep
10:35–11: 25	Co-Teach	Co-Teach	Co-Teach	Indirect Support	Co-Teach
11:30–12:05	Lunch	Lunch	Lunch	Lunch	Lunch
12:15–1:05	Co-Teach	Co-Teach	Co-Teach	Indirect Support	Co-Teach
1:10–2:00	Co-Teach	Co-Teach	Co-Teach	Indirect Support	Co-Teach
2:05–2:55	Learning Center	Learning Center	Learning Center	Learning Center	Learning Center

TO SUM UP

- Effective co-teaching with a special educator involves using several models. Though the Duet Model is the best, it may not be realistic due to its time requirements. Other models that work well include Skill Groups, Learning Style, and Complementary.

- Special educators who co-teach must be vigilant about their responsibilities to address IEP objectives within the context of the classroom instruction. Special educators may need to be assertive in planning meetings to ensure that they are being fully utilized and meeting student needs.

DISCUSSION QUESTIONS

- Several legal mandates must be considered when general and special education teachers co-teach. What are these mandates and how might they affect the co-teaching process?

- How does the role of the special education teacher differ from the general education teacher in a co-taught class?

- Imagine you are an observer in a class co-taught by a special education and a general education teacher. What might it look like?

CHAPTER 15

Co-Teaching with a Speech/Language Pathologist

Imagine that you are a successful baseball player—a veteran with many years of experience and success under your belt. You have received trophies and recognition for your numerous winning seasons. Suddenly, you are told that the rules of the game have changed. There will be two additional players on the field at all times, your playbook will be public knowledge, and after two strikes, the batter gets to choose a teammate to coach him.

This analogy seems fitting to the changes taking place in Speech and Language services in public education. For years, speech/language pathologists were successful at following the rules they played by in school settings:

The "Old Rules"

- Students who need speech and language services should be pulled out to a quiet environment for one-on-one instruction.

- Speech and Language Pathologists (SLPs) are trained in a medical model and will not be able to generalize their skills to a classroom setting and core curriculum areas.

- Speech services need to be provided in a separate space to avoid disrupting the classroom.

Several changes have occurred in recent years that have caused a reexamination of the way speech and language services have been provided. Changes in federal mandates regarding the Least Restrictive Environment (LRE) now require greater access to general education curriculum. Speech as a pull-out service is now being reconsidered in light of stricter accountability for LRE.

Response to Intervention (RtI) is a process for making educational decisions about students who are struggling. Once a student is identified as being at-risk for learning difficulties, RtI provides a research-based, tiered intervention system with increasing levels of intensity and duration. RtI is largely used as a process for identifying learning disabilities in the reading area, but can also be effective for early identification of speech and language difficulties. Kami Jessop, an inclusion facilitator and SLP for Papillion LaVista School District in Nebraska, believes that SLPs have a unique opportunity as co-teachers:

> An SLP can serve as an RTI interventionist—watching for red flags, for delays in expressive and receptive language that have not yet been identified. SLPs who are co-teaching might see things that a general education teacher might not pick up on. We have to know about communication in all forms—while general education teachers tend to think of it as oral or written. SLPs also notice the use of gestures, facial expression, tone of voice and body language. Because of this perspective, we might see issues or weaknesses that the classroom teacher might miss.

College preparatory programs are also changing. Dr. Catherine Crowley, Distinguished Lecturer from Teachers College at Columbia University, reports that close to 100 percent of master's degree SLP programs around the country have coursework in literacy (personal communication, November, 2010). Special education administrators report that new SLP graduates seem to have a greater understanding of literacy and some of the specific methodologies such as guided reading. SLPs have the skills to collaborate with school professionals to assist in developing programs for emergent literacy and literacy skills among general education students as well as students who have identified spoken language and literacy problems.

The American Speech-Language-Hearing Association (ASHA) released a policy statement (2010) emphasizing the need for changes in service delivery:

> School-based speech-language pathology is at a crossroads where SLPs seek to contribute significantly to the well-being and success of children and adolescents in schools as ever-increasing demands are placed on

them with an expanded scope of practice. It is essential that SLPs' roles and responsibilities be redefined in light of substantive changes that have taken place in schools.

What might these new rules look like?

The "New Rules"

- Students who need speech and language services also need to interact linguistically with age-appropriate role models.

- Speech and Language Pathologists are trained in language and literacy and the importance of generalizing these skills to all walks of life.

- Speech services provided in the general education classroom benefit an even greater number of students than just those with IEPs.

As SLPs adjust to these new "rules," they are finding that co-teaching is an effective structure for providing their services in a more inclusive manner. The benefits of collaborative service delivery in the speech and language arena include

- Innovative solutions

- Development of functional communication skills in valid contexts

- Generalization of targeted skills

- Increased motivation of staff through professional interactions

These benefits confirm what practitioners already know—inclusive, collaborative service delivery makes good sense.

Best Models

The caseloads of SLPs are usually much larger than other specialists—fifty students is not unusual. The caseload size will have a large impact on which co-teaching models can be used. School districts are encouraged to consider the SLP's workload in light of the goals they are trying to achieve. Adding co-teaching to an already overwhelming workload will not yield the desired results. Instead, administrators and SLPs will want to discuss creative ways to design class rosters and schedules to ensure that co-teaching can occur effectively and efficiently.

The most common model used by SLPs is the Complementary Skills Model. In this model, the teacher shares the general curriculum outline and daily lesson plans with the specialist. The specialist looks for opportunities within the course of the content to infuse a mini-lesson that addresses the speech and language needs of the students in the class. For example, if a kindergarten teacher will be introducing the letter "P" to her students, the SLP might prepare visuals for how the mouth looks when it is forming the letter "P," and weave in a brief exercise for all the students that involves articulating the sound while looking in a mirror. At the secondary level, the specialist might look for lesson content that would lend itself well to debate, and then present a mini-lesson on techniques that help to maintain focus during stressful verbal interactions. In both of these examples, the SLP is providing instruction aimed at meeting a student's IEP objectives, but within the large group context in a way that may benefit all students in the class.

> *The specialist looks for opportunities within the content to infuse a mini-lesson that addresses the speech and language needs of the students in the class.*

For a more powerful punch, the SLP might take the lead for an entire classroom period. For example, Terri Spencer, an SLP, and her co-teacher identified a component of their school communication curriculum for which the therapist could take the lead. To save time, Spencer then planned the specifics of the lesson on her own and e-mailed the lesson outline to the classroom teacher.

The Station Teaching Model is also commonly used in collaboration between SLPs and general education teachers. This model allows a greater intensity of service to the targeted students in the classroom. Typically, the lesson will begin with whole group instruction, led by the classroom teacher while the SLP offers support. When the lesson shifts into an application activity, the SLP will invite a small number of students to join her at a station off to the side or back of the room. The majority of these students will have IEP objectives for speech and language, but the group may also include some students who can serve as language role models. The SLP will

EXHIBIT 15.1: Co-Taught Lesson with an SLP

Class: Communication Lab

ELA Standard: Speaking/Listening

> 1a. Initiate and participate effectively in a range of collaborative discussions
>
> Objective: students will identify and apply the elements of effective praise

Warm-Up

SLP: Choose four kids and praise them. Give generic praise to two of the students. Then give specific praise to the other two students.

Teacher: Ask the two kids who received generic praise what they did that was so good. Some students may guess that they were listening or paying attention. Ask them if they are sure that's what they did that was good. They'll have to say, "No" because the praise wasn't specific

SLP: Ask them if they can repeat their behavior. With puzzled faces, again they'll have to say, "No."

Then we'll repeat the same process and explain that because these students received specific praise, they could repeat that good behavior again if they wished.

Teacher: Ask students, "What does 'specific' mean?"

SLP: Explain that in Com Lab today they are going to learn how to send specific praise so our friends, teachers, and parents know what they are doing that we like.

then facilitate a learning activity that parallels the rest of the class, but allows her to intensify her support to the targeted students. The smaller group size ensures greater student participation and teacher monitoring.

Challenges

SLPs travel from class to class, carrying with them a wealth of expertise that can benefit students. Unfortunately, many general education teachers are not familiar with the talents and skills that SLPs have to offer. Some teachers may view them as having a very limited role—similar to the "old rules"—of pulling students out of the class for articulation exercises. Add to this the fact that many SLPs work with several schools and will be unable to attend faculty meetings, eat lunch in the faculty lounge, or chat with colleagues after school. Instead of the strong bonding that often happens between teachers in a building as they get to know each other well, SLPs may experience a very weak connection with these colleagues. The challenge for SLPs is to advocate for themselves, explaining the gifts they have to offer, and to gently massage a paradigm shift for the teachers. Rapport-building efforts in the early stages, such as finding common interests or asking about family, will yield great long-term results.

> *The challenge for SLPs is to advocate for themselves, explaining the gifts they have to offer, and to gently massage a paradigm shift for the teachers.*

Although college programs have prepared SLPs with knowledge and skills in language and literacy, they have not received the same training as teachers. This may become evident if SLPs are assigned to co-teach in content areas such as mathematics, science, or history. Some specialists may feel intimidated by unknown content and assume a more passive role in that classroom. To avoid this problem, SLPs should advocate for the best venues in which to provide the services their students need.

Large-group behavior management skills may also cause some SLPs anxiety. Though teachers have opportunities to learn these skills in their college programs, most SLPs do not. Their practicum experience usually involves working with small groups or one-on-one.

Tackling whole-class behavior management can be frightening at times for even a veteran teacher! Co-teaching partners will want to discuss comfort levels with these responsibilities and allow for a period of growth before fully sharing all roles. This can be a wonderful chance for the general education teacher to share his philosophy of behavior and classroom management and model strategies. Reflective conversations can then occur which allow the specialist to react to the strategies she has seen and offer ideas for tweaking the strategies to better support students with language deficits.

Essential for Success

The availability of professional development opportunities is essential for SLPs' success in co-teaching. If they feel that quality training in topics such as classroom management is available, they will be more willing to embrace their new role as co-teacher. Of course, this holds true for all co-teachers who may feel unprepared to teach a subject area or large group of students. While co-teaching embraces the fact that the teaching partners have different expertise, it should also support a minimum comfort level for all involved.

The principle of natural proportions suggests inclusion is most successful when classes are composed of students that mirror the natural makeup of the community at large. In other words, students with disabilities or other issues of concern should be spread evenly across all classrooms so that no single class is overwhelmed. Though this is ideal, it is not very realistic from a staffing perspective. Natural proportions would mean that specialists would be spread thinly across many classrooms, running from place to place for brief periods of time. This is especially true for SLPs, whose caseloads are often twice or three times that of special education teachers. In order to turn co-teaching into a reality for SLPs, administrators will need to consider clustering students with speech and language difficulties into fewer classrooms. If there are six second graders identified as needing services, it will be much more possible for the SLP to co-teach if they are all placed in one classroom rather than divided among three classrooms.

Even when cluster grouping has been used, it may not be possible for the SLP to co-teach five days per week in a classroom. It will be essential that teachers understand the workload of the SLP and participate in collaborative problem solving when designing the schedule. The team might decide that the SLP will co-teach on Monday, Wednesday, and Friday one week, then Tuesday and Thursday the next week, flip-flopping with another class. Or perhaps the SLP will co-teach two days per week, determined by the curriculum design. For example, if there is a pattern to the curriculum—vocabulary is usually introduced on Mondays, and Thursday is typically a small-group application day—then the team may choose these as the best days for co-teaching. The key is for general education teachers and SLPs to think creatively and flexibly about how to accomplish their goals.

TO SUM UP

- In the past it was common for SLPs to pull students out of classrooms to provide services. Now most services are offered within the classroom so that appropriate role models are available and skills can be applied to real contexts immediately.

- Co-teaching with an SLP will usually involve the Complementary Skills Model or the Station Teaching Model. Because of large caseloads, co-teaching may not occur on a daily basis. Therefore, partners will want to plan for the strongest impact possible in their time together.

DISCUSSION QUESTIONS

- How have the rules for delivery of SLP services changed over time?
- SLPs typically have very large caseloads. How will this affect the co-teaching arrangement?
- Imagine a classroom in which the SLP is using the Complementary Skills Model to co-teach. What might both teachers be doing during her mini-lesson?

CHAPTER 16

Co-Teaching with an Occupational or Physical Therapist

Several years ago, a ski accident resulted in four breaks in my right leg. Midnight surgery was followed by casting, a quick lesson on safe crutch use, and several weeks of boring bed rest. Eventually, the surgeon faxed a referral to a physical therapy practice in the office next door for biweekly therapy sessions. After six weeks the physical therapist faxed a progress report back to the surgeon. Several months later, still experiencing significant pain and mobility issues, it was time to see the surgeon again. X-rays showed that the bones had healed, and the surgeon declared his role finished. Limping out of the office, down the hallway, past the physical therapy office, I had to wonder if there was a better way.

Occupational and physical therapy services originated as part of a medical model. This approach could be described as multidisciplinary—several disciplines involved in the process of healing or correcting a problem. Each member of a multidisciplinary team brings a unique skill set and perspective to the problem. While communication occurs between disciplines, it is not often face-to-face or extensive communication. In some cases, usually the simple ones, the multidisciplinary approach is enough. But when problems are complex, the multidisciplinary approach often fails.

Struggling students in inclusive educational settings present a complex set of needs that challenge us to move beyond the multidisciplinary model for the delivery of occupational and physical therapy (OT/PT) services. What works in the medical field doesn't translate well to the educational field. Instead, a transdisciplinary approach is a more effective solution. The prefix "trans" means "across." In transdisciplinary teaming, professionals from different disciplines work much more closely together to cross traditional disciplinary boundaries and collaboratively design and implement an individualized education plan. The OT/PT no longer works with the student in a separate space, but integrates his expertise into the classroom setting.

The most effective application of this transdisciplinary approach in education is co-teaching.

IDEA encourages co-teaching for OTs and PTs. It defines "related services" as being services required to assist a child with a disability to benefit from education. As nationally recognized OT Tere Bowen-Irish writes, "OTs need training that focuses on school-based delivery services that are collaborative in nature. The fact that we have only been in education for 34 years puts us at a disadvantage. Each year is bringing more insight and application" (personal communication, 2011). If the goal of therapy services truly is to help a student access and benefit from their education, it is crucial for the therapist to participate in the setting where that education is taking place.

> *If the goal of therapy services truly is to help a student access and benefit from their education, it is crucial for the therapist to participate in the setting where that education is taking place.*

In addition, IDEA encourages co-teaching through its provisions for Least Restrictive Environment (LRE). The law requires that children with disabilities be educated with children who are nondisabled to the maximum extent appropriate. Removal from general education classes is only allowed when the education cannot be achieved satisfactorily **with the use of supplementary aids and services.** This provision implies that OT/PT services should be attempted in the regular class before pull-out services are determined to be necessary.

Best Models

Any of the models that allow for small-group work lend themselves well to co-teaching with an OT or PT. This would include the Skill Groups, Station Teaching, or Parallel models. In the small-group setting, the therapist can work with the targeted student(s) with enough intensity to satisfy their therapeutic goals, and yet still provide a context of nondisabled peers.

As with other co-teaching partnerships, the best end result is achieved when the teammates begin with collaborative planning. The classroom teacher may present the curricular goals and the intended lesson plan. The therapist can then suggest adaptations to the plan that will address the therapeutic objectives while simultaneously making education more accessible (see Table 16.1).

TABLE 16.1: Co-Taught Lesson with an OT

GENERAL PLAN—KINDERGARTEN MATH—MR. JENNINGS	OT ADAPTATIONS TO PLAN—MRS. BOWEN-IRISH
Students will be rotating through math centers. 1. Counting math cubes by tens 2. Matching game with squares, circles, rectangles 3. Distributing pizza slices 4. Sorting photos by season	*Bina and Torrie's goals can be worked into center #1. Let's provide chopsticks to the students and have them place the cubes into a bowl as they are counting. This will work on muscle strength for pencil grip. I will sit at this station.*

While occupational and physical therapy goals may be woven into many of aspects of a student's school day, subjects such as art and physical education can be especially accommodating. Because these teachers already provide frequent tactile and kinesthetic activities, it is easy to incorporate therapeutic movement (see Table 16.2).

TABLE 16.2: Co-Taught Lesson with a PT

PHYSICAL EDUCATION—5TH GRADE—MRS. CONLIN	PT ADAPTATIONS TO PLAN—MR. LEE
Spelling Word Relay Teams ✛ Individual Stretching Basketball Cool Down and Fitness Logs	*Kyle will join a team and use his motorized wheelchair. Can we have students use stretching partners? I will trio with Kyle and his partner to work on his range of motion.* *During the game I'll work with Kyle on passing to his left. One of his goals is to perform cool down exercises independently.*

✛ See Appendix A

After the instruction phase is complete, the therapist is on the move to the next location. Collaborative grading is unlikely to occur when co-teaching with a therapist. The therapist will usually assume the responsibility for reporting about progress on IEP objectives related to motor skills, whereas the classroom teacher handles other assessment decisions.

Challenges

Due to the low incidence of students requiring OT/PT services, therapists are usually itinerant, traveling from school to school in the course of a single day. They are often employed by an outside agency, rather than the school district. Questions about scheduling, supervision, responsibilities, and caseloads can be complicated and exacerbate a disconnectedness between the co-teachers. As Bowen-Irish states (personal communication, 2010), "Therapists are so spread out that it is hard to develop chemistry. Teachers usually see your rear end leaving to run to another school. In the ideal world the therapist would be on staff and be able to connect with the staff and learn the curriculum."

Although it is unlikely schools will have budgets to hire full-time OTs and PTs, the administration can turn their awareness of this disconnectedness into corrective action. One school principal arranged to hold monthly staff meetings on an afternoon when therapists were scheduled to be in the building. He placed issues specifically related to them first on the agenda so that they could participate for a few minutes, without adding significantly to their time commitment in the building.

Scheduling challenges make it difficult enough to arrange common planning time for two professionals who share a building site all week long; the schedules of itinerant therapists make weekly common planning time close to impossible. Without common planning time, it becomes much more difficult to share responsibilities. Anyone partnering with an itinerant therapist will need to accept the major responsibility for lesson planning, and give the therapist permission to tweak the plan to meet student needs. Other responsibilities, such as grading, classroom management, and handling daily routines, will necessarily fall under the purview of the classroom teacher.

When co-teachers do not have time to engage in conversation and get to know each other, misconceptions can be common. Classroom teachers may only think of occupational therapists as handwriting experts, and not realize the wide array of other skills they bring to the table. Teachers may be anxious that physical therapists will rile up students with lots of activity, and then move on to their next appointment, leaving the classroom in chaos. The challenge for therapists will be to educate their partners about the talents they can contribute to enrich the learning experience for all students.

Essential for Success

Most people who choose to work in school settings don't consider themselves to be good at sales. They may say they don't have a head for business or don't like trying to sell others on an idea or a product. Itinerant therapists will be most successful in co-teaching if they can overcome this hesitation and sell themselves. Consider for a moment how excited a teacher might be to learn that her co-teaching therapist can add an unexpected breadth and depth to her bag of classroom strategies. Consider for a moment how relieved a teacher might be to hear that her co-teaching therapist has the skills and knowledge necessary to work within the curriculum, rather than adding extraneous, unconnected activities. A therapist who sells herself—the talents and ideas that make her a valuable, desirable asset—will find herself working with an enthusiastic partner.

> *A therapist who sells herself—the talents and ideas that make her a valuable, desirable asset—will find herself working with an enthusiastic partner.*

In order for a therapist to feel comfortable selling her ability to make classroom connections, it is essential that she have at least a general understanding of the curriculum standards at each grade level. For example, it will be discouraging for all involved if a therapist comes to class not knowing that first graders are expected to manipulate and understand coins. Most college programs do not provide this type of detailed information. Therefore, therapists may need professional development workshops to help them become acquainted with the district's common standards. It will also be an enormous help if therapists have easy access to a copy of curriculum guides, student texts, or relevant concept maps. The expectation is not that the therapists should know these materials inside and out, but that they have a familiarity that makes it possible to effectively integrate therapeutic and academic objectives.

TO SUM UP

- Occupational and Physical Therapists will find it most effective to co-teach using any of the models that include small group work. Models such as Skill Groups, Station, or Parallel will allow the therapist to provide the intense, direct instruction needed by just a few targeted students.

- Classroom teachers may need to assist their partners in understanding the curriculum content and standards. Therapists may not have a comprehensive background in curriculum, but will be able to integrate their expertise if their co-teaching partners collaboratively brainstorm ideas.

DISCUSSION QUESTIONS

- What are some of the unique challenges that occur when an occupational or physical therapist co-teaches with a general educator?
- Which co-teaching models will make the most sense? Why?
- Picture a typical school day. What learning activities might best lend themselves to co-teaching with an occupational or physical therapist?

CHAPTER 17

Co-Teaching with a Paraeducator

Mr. Nedd, a solid, fire hydrant of a man, straddles a chair in front of the room and looks out at twenty-nine faces filled with anticipation. The students know that Mr. Nedd is a gifted storyteller, and straddling a chair is his cue that a story is coming their way.

Ms. Spinoza silently surfs the room, cuing a student to turn her body to face Mr. Nedd, cuing another student to sit on his beach ball seat. While Mr. Nedd's story will be captivating, a few students will be challenged by the length of it. Ms. Spinoza knows that it will be critical to the application assignment that students stay attentive.

Which adult is the paraeducator?

Paraeducators, also known as teacher aides, instructional assistants, and paraprofessionals, play an important role in inclusive classrooms by supporting the learning opportunities presented by classroom teachers. As classroom membership has become more and more heterogeneous, paraeducators have become more common in general education settings. Rather than pulling individual students out into hallways or down to a special room, paraeducators are being welcomed as an integral part of the classroom community.

Unfortunately, "welcomed" does not necessarily translate into "effectively utilized." Wolf Wolfensberger once defined inclusion as "True inclusion is **valued** participation, in **valued** activities, in **valued** settings" (1983). Although he was referring to individuals with disabilities, the same notion applies to paraeducators in the classroom. Simply placing a second adult in the room will not result in added value to learning. It is critical that the teacher works closely with the paraeducator to develop a valuable role in every aspect of the instructional cycle. Co-teaching, with its emphasis on coordination and communication, will optimize the talents that the paraeducator brings to the setting.

> *It is critical that the teacher works closely with the paraeducator to develop a valuable role in every aspect of the instructional cycle.*

Shaping the Role of the Paraeducator

Several questions will help in shaping the role of the paraeducator as a co-teacher.

- What training and experience does the paraeducator bring to the class?
  Under NCLB, paraeducators are required to meet certain qualifications. Most paraeducators have skills that far surpass the minimum requirements. Conversations that identify these skills, talents, and interests will provide fodder for lesson planning. (In our example, Mr. Nedd, a paraeducator, is a phenomenal storyteller. His co-teachers tap into this talent whenever possible.)

- Why has the paraeducator been assigned to this class?
  Some paraeducators have been hired to support reading intervention programs, while others have been hired as "one-on-one" aides for students with severe behavior disorders. Some paraeducators have been hired to help in primary grades with large class sizes, while others offer all-purpose special education support. The answer to this question will have a strong impact on how the paraeducator can be utilized as a co-teacher.

- Is the paraeducator being shared with other classes?
  As with any other co-teaching partner, the amount of time that a paraeducator has to devote to co-teaching in a specific classroom will affect the quality of what can be accomplished. Unlike a special education or reading teacher, there may be

greater flexibility in the paraeducator's schedule. If so, it will serve all classes well if the classroom teachers who work with a common paraeducator collaborate and communicate about her schedule. For example, when a special activity arises in one class, the other teachers can be flexible to accommodate a schedule change that allows the paraeducator to help with the special activity.

Best Models

In the past, the most common model for co-teaching with a paraeducator was the Adapting Model. The paraeducator would either sit next to a targeted student or roam the room, offering adaptations when necessary. This version of co-teaching is questionable. Does this fully utilize the second adult? Probably not. Yet most paraeducators are not certified teachers and cannot assume major instructional responsibilities. Because of this, some teachers have fallen into the habit of using paraeducators in limited ways.

Fortunately, other educators have a different outlook and are beginning to see a panorama of options. The Speak and Add Model provides wonderful opportunities for a paraeducator to increase his or her involvement in a classroom. The benefits of differing voices, differing personalities, differing perspectives are all enhanced when a second adult can jump in and add to the lesson. As an observer in a high school biology class, I witnessed the simple beauty of this firsthand. A paraeducator had been assigned to the class to support a student with autism. Rather than sitting next to the targeted student, she roamed his half of the room, allowing him opportunities to experience independence or use peers as resources. During the teacher's lecture, the paraeducator sat facing the class, typing notes into a computer that was projected onto a screen. These notes served as a model for the whole class, but also became the lecture notes for the targeted student. At one point during the lecture, the biology teacher wanted to real aloud a list of items. Instead of reading by himself, the teacher asked the paraeducator to read every other item. The varying vocal qualities kept all the students more engaged in listening (and me, as well!).

Any of the models which employ small-group work may also be effective when co-teaching with a paraeducator, as long as the groups are used for application activities rather than initial instruction. With direction, paraeducators can facilitate half of the class in a Parallel Model, using an activity that has been designed by the classroom teacher. In the example shown in Table 17.1, the paraeducator facilitates half of the class during two separate activities, both of short duration. The classroom teacher is still present in case any content questions arise that require her expertise.

TABLE 17.1: Co-Taught Lesson with a Paraeducator

Objective: Activating prior knowledge and connections	
MRS. MATHERS—CLASSROOM TEACHER	MRS. ZHANG—PARAEDUCATOR
Check in with students upon arrival Split into two groups for The Answer Is . . . (five minutes) followed by three minutes of dialogue on "What do you notice about your questions?" Back together as whole group for mini-lecture Four stations for hands-on exploration	Put out butcher paper and markers Take one group for The Answer Is . . . —Cheng and Seiko will be in your group Complete graphic organizer on board during lecture Monitor two of four stations

See Appendix A

Challenges

The role of a paraeducator in a co-taught classroom is much more limited than that of other professional partners. Typically, a paraeducator will not be able to participate in grading decisions, parent conferences, planning instructional goals and activities, and many other professional responsibilities. The burden for these tasks will rest on the teacher's shoulders. However, there are dozens of other ways that a paraeducator can be utilized. The challenge is for the teacher to identify these opportunities, ensure that the paraeducator knows what to do and is doing the tasks correctly.

Confusion about paraeducator supervision is common. Most teachers do not view themselves as supervisors, and may feel uncomfortable in the role. College programs do not usually teach the skills needed for effective supervision of other adults. Add to this hesitance the fact that a paraeducator may be directed by a specialist, several classroom teachers, and a principal, and role confusion is bound to occur. Taking time to delineate these responsibilities will be worthwhile. Consider the following scenario:

A special education paraeducator is assigned to support Mia, a student with multiple disabilities, during her language arts and math blocks in third grade. Her classroom teacher has had limited experience with students so significantly disabled and has twenty-seven other students to teach.

> *Confusion about paraeducator supervision is common.*

Who is responsible for guiding the paraeducator? The answer is complex. The special education teacher is responsible for providing guidance in specialized techniques to help Mia learn. Other specialists—the speech, occupational, and physical therapists that work with Mia—are responsible for showing the paraeducator any appropriate strategies related to goals in their domains. But the classroom teacher is responsible for guiding and supervising the paraeducator when these other professionals aren't present. The classroom teacher will be able to create ways to include Mia in the curriculum activities and see moment-by-moment chances to integrate her individualized objectives.

From the paraeducator's perspective, directions from so many sources can be confusing, frustrating, and overwhelming. Combine this with the fact that paraeducators often work in multiple classrooms with multiple professionals, and the communication network may become a tangled mess. A high school paraeducator lamented, "I work with five teachers with five different personalities. Sometimes it feels like I am at one of those complicated traffic circles with different on and off ramps and I have to find the right speed to merge safely."

Essential for Success

A communication and supervision plan is crucial for co-teaching with a paraeducator. The most effective plan will be developed in a meeting in which all of the team members are present. Roles and responsibilities can be discussed and delineated so that everyone is on the same page. The paraeducator can ask clarifying questions and have follow-up steps for what to do if future confusion occurs.

In order to do this, common planning time is necessary. If a paraeducator is assigned full-time to one classroom, then collaborative planning can occur during one or more of the teacher's prep periods. If working with several teachers, it is common for the paraeducator to be assigned to another class during the teacher's prep. To make this even more difficult, paraeducators often work the same hours that students are in the building, which makes before- or after-school communication seem impossible. Some administrators have solved this problem by allowing flexible scheduling once per week. The paraeducator will arrive thirty minutes early for collaborative planning and then be released thirty minutes early on that same day. Creative thinking like this will lead to teaming with positive results.

Former special education teacher Jacquie Knight has many years of experience co-teaching with paraeducators and is now a private school administrator in California. Her advice for success is simple: "Forming a relationship is essential so that you can present yourselves as a team to the students. Take the time to get to know your paraeducator" (personal communication, 2010). Knowledge of a partner's strengths allows you to capitalize on these when designing lessons, giving him or her a more active role in educating all students.

Collaborative, synergistic relationships are the goal for co-teachers. However, there are times when the teacher may need to step into a hierarchical relationship with the paraeducator. If a paraeducator has misunderstood a direction and is incorrectly reinforcing a skill, the teacher must step in. If a paraeducator believes her own approach will work best and is not following the teacher's direction, the teacher must step in. The responsibility for supervision must be accepted for the sake of the students. When a teacher is uncomfortable with this role, it is often due to a lack of confidence and supervision skills. Workshops or coaching on these missing skills will ensure that the co-teaching relationship remains healthy while addressing the needs of students.

TO SUM UP

- Although paraeducators may not be as comprehensively involved in a co-taught classroom as a professional educator, there are still myriad ways to utilize them effectively.

- The responsibility for guiding and supervising a paraeducator usually falls to the professional educator most often present in the classroom. Teachers may need some professional development to help them become comfortable with this role.

DISCUSSION QUESTIONS

- What roles can a paraeducator adopt in a co-taught classroom to be more fully utilized?

- How might a teacher find time to communicate and plan with a paraeducator?

- Supervision of a paraeducator can be complex. Which professionals might be involved in supervision? What issues might affect this process?

CHAPTER 18

Co-Teaching with a Gifted Specialist

Inclusive education is supported in principle by most thoughtful adults. However, once inclusion is put into practice, these same adults might raise concerns. Consider the following scenario.

A One-Act Play with a Happy Ending

The Setting: A middle school auditorium; about fifty parents seated near the front; the school principal just finishing a multimedia presentation on his school's inclusive practices.

Parent #1: I appreciate what you are trying to accomplish, but . . . I have a son who is gifted and needs to be challenged, not held back by kids who are struggling.

Parent #2: Me, too. What are you doing about the smart kids?

Many audience members' heads nod.

Principal: Great question. Our teachers have been participating in extensive training in how to teach to the broad array of children in their classes. In addition, we have had a pilot program of co-teaching this semester. Co-teaching allows our gifted specialist to work in the classroom, collaborating with the classroom teacher. They are integrating higher-order thinking skills into their daily lessons.

Parent #1: I can't picture that. Can you give me an example?

Principal: Better than that! I've invited our gifted and social studies co-teachers here tonight to share with you some of their successes.

A teacher passes out a handout to the audience with the following list of strategies, and then the partners describe their application in the classroom. A sense of relief emanates from the audience.

- Bloom's Connection Puzzles ⊞
- Challenge Authority Cards ⊞
- RAFTs ⊞
- The Back of a Napkin ⊞
- Individual Contracts
- Sticky Situations

⊞ See Appendix A

According to the National Association for Gifted Children (NAGC), approximately 3,000,000 gifted children are present in U.S. classrooms. The potential they represent is staggering. Unfortunately, that potential is often not realized. Students who are gifted have the same high school dropout rate as the rest of the population. In addition, students who are identified in preschool and kindergarten as showing advanced levels of thinking often level out by fourth grade to be on grade level. One study shows that the majority of classroom teachers have no training in strategies for teaching gifted students and make only minor modifications for the gifted students in their classrooms (Archambault et al., 1993).

NAGC advocates for a continuum of programming options for gifted children, including collaboration. Its position statement titled "Collaboration between Gifted and General Education Programs" affirms the power of collaborative models:

> Collaboration among gifted, general, and special education professionals is essential in order to meet the special needs of all students. Collaborative environments foster communication, cooperation, and shared responsibility for gifted and general education students among all school staff, and encourage communication and cooperation among educators. Through collaborative efforts, teachers share their expertise and insights as they plan for their students, regardless of the

nature of the program in which they specialize. Collaboration enhances understanding and trust among fields of education, helps promote connections between services in all educational fields, helps develop more positive attitudes toward gifted education, and increases opportunities for students. (NAGC, 1993)

These opportunities apply to all students in a classroom setting. When the gifted specialist uses her expertise to co-plan a lesson, all class members can benefit. Carol Richert, a gifted specialist in Elkhorn, Nebraska, found that co-teaching allowed her to be inclusive. Richert confirms these benefits: "Teachers often identified students who they felt were bright but whose test scores were not high enough to make them eligible for gifted programs. By working in the classroom, I could include all students in the techniques I employed" (personal communication, 2010).

Best Models

Many educators and parents are calling for federal mandates and funding for gifted education. Until this occurs, staffing for gifted specialists is likely to continue to be sparse. The typical elementary school may only have a gifted specialist for a few hours each day, shared amongst all of the classes. The Complementary skills Model will have the most powerful effect, given the time constraints of the gifted specialist.

Gerald Aungst, currently a supervisor of gifted education in Cheltenham, Pennsylvania, frequently used the Complementary Skills Model as a co-teacher. Meeting briefly with the general education teacher, he would examine the upcoming lessons to spark ideas for integrating higher-order skills into the traditional curriculum. For example, Aungst co-taught in a first-grade class that had a cluster of three students identified as gifted. With a complicated schedule, he found that the only time he could join the class was when science activities were scheduled. He and his co-teacher would take whatever was planned for that day and adapt the lesson to include challenges for the gifted students, as well as the rest of the class. An example of these types of adaptations is shown in Table 18.1.

TABLE 18.1: Co-Taught Lesson with a Gifted Specialist—Elementary

Living and Nonliving Things	
GENERAL APPROACH	COMPLEMENTARY HIGHER-ORDER THINKING SKILLS
What is a living thing? What is a nonliving thing? Discussion, Venn diagram, props, pictures Sticky labels—partners label items in room	Introduce vocabulary, "natural" and "man-made," generate other terms Design bar graph for living and nonliving things found in the room Lead a metacognition check

Many gifted specialists find the Skill Groups Model to be applicable to their co-teaching goals. The Skill Groups Model will allow the specialist to work directly with students who are ready for greater complexity, providing them with an intensity of direct instruction that may be harder to achieve in a whole-group Complementary Skills Model. Gifted specialists often report that this model feels like a more deliberate, concentrated delivery of service to the gifted students. The grouping arrangements for this can vary to include:

- Splitting the class into two groups by ability level with the topic. The gifted specialist can work with those ready for greater complexity, while the general education teacher works with the rest of the class to solidify their understanding. Both teachers develop their own lessons.

- Splitting the class into three groups by ability level with the topic. The gifted specialist works with those ready for greater complexity. The students on grade-level work independently on an anchor activity. The struggling students work with the classroom teacher.

- Developing two or more station activities. Students travel in ability-based groups from one station to another. The gifted specialist works at one station and enriches the discussion and learning when the more advanced students are with her. See Table 18.2.

Whichever arrangement is chosen, teachers will want to be sure to design activities that are engaging for all students so that none feel left out, bored, or ignored.

TABLE 18.2: Co-Taught Lesson with a Gifted Specialist—Secondary

World War II—Japanese American Internment Camps	
MR. VEGA—SOCIAL STUDIES TEACHER	**MRS. RICHERT—GIFTED SPECIALIST**
Internment Camps—mini-lecture Internet site tour Break into four groups and have students start their rotations through stations (should take 4–5 days) Station A: You Lose Bingo Game  (simulate the losses experienced by Japanese Americans) Station B: Multiple Perspective Glasses 	Add higher level questions during mini-lecture Station C: Webquest  activity—independent but monitored Station D: Virtual Tug-of-War Debate —facilitated

 See Appendix A

Challenges

Myths about gifted students abound. Overcoming these can be one of the biggest hurdles to co-teaching. A prevalent myth is that gifted students will do just fine on their own in the general education classroom. Overworked teachers often feel that they need to make tough choices about which students in their classes get extra attention—and gifted students rarely are the chosen ones. Gifted specialist Aungst shares that some of his co-teachers initially wondered how taking an hour per week to focus on higher-level thinking was going to help test scores: "The teachers that were willing to take the leap found that it benefited all the kids in the class. A lot of techniques and thought processes really began to crystallize for them and led to them implementing the techniques throughout the rest of the week" (personal communication, 2010).

Once classroom teachers have had the opportunity to co-teach with a gifted specialist, they often crave more—more time to co-plan, more chances to co-teach. But the reality in most schools is that gifted specialists will have very limited time. Until federal minimum standards for gifted education are passed, local funding will be

"Once classroom teachers have had the opportunity to co-teach with a gifted specialist, they often crave more—more time to co-plan, more chances to co-teach."

limited and inadequate. The challenge for partners will be to choose the richest periods of the day and mine them for every chance to integrate higher level thinking skills.

Essential for Success

Discussions about "collaboration" usually involve phrases such as "coequal parties" and "shared decision making." These concepts make up the gold standard for co-teaching—a sense of parity and balance between partners. However, when one partner, out of scheduling necessity, must operate as a visiting teacher, the balance in the partnership usually shifts. This is true in the case of the gifted specialist who may be co-teaching with someone just once per week. It will fall to the specialist to be the more flexible partner in the relationship. Gifted specialists who experience co-teaching success often speak about developing rapport in the early stages by meeting the classroom teacher wherever she was, rather than coming into the relationship with all kinds of premade plans and agendas. This willingness to blend into the preexisting picture will save time and result in a more enthusiastic welcome from the classroom teacher. Carol Richert, a gifted specialist in Elkhorn, Nebraska, put it this way: "The first time I co-taught with a teacher, I tried to find out what the teacher wanted or needed. What were her concerns? What areas of higher level thinking intrigued her? After we planned a lesson, I offered to gather all the materials we needed—to take on some of the hassle so that it wouldn't seem a burden. Over time, I felt less of a need to do this as my partners saw the value I could bring to the classroom" (personal communication, 2010).

In some schools gifted education will include a continuum of services. It may be deemed appropriate for some students to receive intensive, pull-out services, as well as co-taught services. Specialists who have worked with students in both types of settings often report that seeing their students function in a regular class environment gives them a much broader perspective on their abilities. Partners should be attuned to the benefits of this type of in-class, functional assessment. It will serve a gifted student best if both of his teachers observe, assess, and address the needs he displays in the heterogeneous classroom. These needs reveal the coping skills he requires to successfully navigate current and future environments.

This type of assessment information may also be helpful during parent-teacher conferences. Many parents want evidence that their child is being appropriately challenged. Parents may need help to see the value of co-teaching. Specific examples of differentiated activities, enrichment, teamwork skills, and creative applications will help parents to feel confident about the program. When partners can co-facilitate parent conferences, communication and support will be greatly enhanced.

TO SUM UP

- Gifted specialists find that the Complementary and the Skill Groups models lend themselves well to meeting the needs of gifted students. This is especially true if the specialist can only co-teach once per week, as these models allow her to be highly focused on enrichment.

- Myths about giftedness may need to be addressed with parents and teachers in order to develop support for a co-teaching program.

DISCUSSION QUESTIONS

- What benefits occur when a gifted specialist co-teaches with a general education teacher?

- What types of grouping activities might work well when co-teaching with a gifted specialist?

- Imagine a lesson plan for co-teaching with a gifted specialist. In which parts of the lesson can you envision her influence? How might the two educators interact throughout the lesson?

CHAPTER 19

Co-Teaching with a Literacy Specialist

Jason was one of several students who began fourth grade labeled as "at-risk." His co-teachers were determined to bring him to grade level in reading and writing by the end of the year. Mrs. Brody, the building's literacy specialist, had witnessed good progress made last year by students in her co-taught classes. She knew that it would require lots of creative planning with the classroom teacher, and flexibility on both parts. They would need to find ways to maintain fidelity to the language arts program the district had adopted, while still differentiating to meet the needs of all students. She was ready for the challenge with a full bag of research-based strategies to share.

Mrs. Brody met with her co-teacher weekly for one planning period. Because they had a prescribed language arts program to follow, their discussions centered mostly on preteaching and reteaching strategies, ways to engage students more kinesthetically, and best grouping arrangements. At times they had to take a specific reading or writing skill and develop a scaffold of small steps for students like Jason. Each planning conversation was rich with ideas, although occasionally stymied by the real-life constraints of a scripted literacy program. But progress was evident, so the partners persevered.

Near the end of the school year, the teachers facilitated a learning unit on metaphorical language. Always one of Mrs. Brody's favorites, she took the lead in developing some hands-on activities to emphasize how metaphors show creative connections. At the end of the metaphor unit Jason approached her with a scrap of paper in his hand. With a big grin on his face, he handed it to Mrs. Brody and said "I wrote this for you." Mrs. Brody grinned big, too, as she read:

Mrs. B is a needle threading strategies through my educational jacket.

Guided reading, scripted teacher manuals, computer-based modules, whole language—literacy specialists may work with any number of approaches to literacy instruction. Each and every one of these approaches can effectively accommodate co-teaching if the co-teachers are flexible and creative. The International Reading Association (IRA) has adopted a policy statement which addresses the role of the literacy specialist in inclusive schools:

> *The range of student achievement found in classrooms, with the inclusion of children who have various physical, emotional, and educational needs, requires that we move to different educational models from those of the past. These new models present opportunities for teachers and reading specialists to work collaboratively to provide effective instruction for all students. . . . In order to promote congruency, collaboration, and communication between classroom teachers and reading specialists, the instruction provided by the reading specialist may take place in the classroom. (IRA, 2000, 1)*

Best Models

Which models work best for co-teaching with a literacy specialist? The answer to this question depends, in part, on the type of literacy program being deployed in the school. Programs that rely heavily on small-group instruction lend themselves well to the Skill Groups Model. In this case, the literacy specialist is most likely to take on the responsibility for planning and implementing instruction for the group of students who is struggling. However, many of the same instructional strategies that might be used with a small group can also be offered through a whole class Complementary Skills Model.

Table 19.1 shows the lesson plan developed by reading specialist Emily Kendig of Huber Heights City Schools in Huber Heights, Ohio. Kendig's fourth grade co-teacher wanted her students to identify examples of cause and effect in text material. In the past, the teacher asked students to practice this skill through the completion of worksheets, but Kendig saw some opportunities for making the concept more accessible.

Kendig acknowledges that different teachers respond well to different models. In some classes she spends more time with the Speak and Add Model, jumping in to clarify or restate, but in other

TABLE 19.1: Co-Taught Lesson with a Literacy Specialist—Elementary

Standard: Identify structural patterns found in informational text (e.g., compare and contrast, cause and effect, sequential or chronological order, proposition and support) to strengthen comprehension.	
MISS K.—READING SPECIALIST	MS. M.—CLASSROOM TEACHER

Show PowerPoint overview of cause/effect
Read aloud *If You Give a Mouse a Cookie*
Explain the If/Then Matching Game—
  students will work in small groups, on the
  floor, matching if-then statements
	Tie examples to prior knowledge
	Emphasize if-then statements
	Both teachers monitor students in their
	  small groups
	Pull class back together and facilitate a
	  reflection on what was learned about
	  cause/effect

classes the teachers share the lead equally, bouncing back and forth depending on the needs of the students. The stronger the rapport she has built with a teacher, the easier it is to switch roles responsively.

In upper grades and secondary schools, students spend increasing amounts of time reading independently. Students may participate in sustained silent reading periods in class, as well as be assigned chapters of fiction or nonfiction texts to read for homework. Initially, co-teachers may not see these activities as ripe for literacy intervention. Here again, the Complementary Skills Model provides a structure for the specialist to utilize their expertise.

Mr. Langley, the literacy specialist, is part of two seventh-grade teams at his middle school. His role is to co-teach in English and social studies classes, looking for ways to strengthen reading skills for all students. One of the things he has noticed in his classes is that some students engage in silent reading with a laser-like focus, while others seem distracted. When he has individual conferences with students, some demonstrate strong recollection and comprehension, while others have great difficulty recalling any details. Mr. Langley shared his observations with his teammates at their weekly team meeting. Impassioned discussion ensued. His English colleagues did not want to do anything to disrupt the natural flow of independent reading. His social studies colleagues were concerned about adding too much reading instruction to their already full class periods. As a group, they developed an idea to model the metacognition that should take place during silent reading. They developed the following Complementary Skills Model lesson to be repeated in English and social studies classes.

TABLE 19.2: Co-Taught Lesson with a Literacy Specialist—Secondary

Objective: Use metacognition to strengthen comprehension and retention of informational text.	
MR. LANGLEY—LITERACY SPECIALIST	**CONTENT TEACHER**
Arrange fishbowl activity—both teachers silent reading while students sit around them watching Begin "thinking aloud about thinking" Define metacognition Distribute and explain Brain Bookmarks Share in debrief	Write objective on board Take turns with Mr. Langley modeling "thinking aloud about thinking" Share connection between metacognition and previous instruction Direct students to read common passage with Brain Bookmarks—then debrief Assign students to use bookmarks for homework

See Appendix A

Challenges

Many schools address their literacy objectives by offering an array of programs and services. This can mean that the literacy specialist wears many different hats throughout the day including teacher, coach, consultant, co-teacher, assessor, curriculum specialist, and staff developer. For the lone literacy specialist in an average-size elementary school, this can feel overwhelming. As one specialist admitted, "It's hard to keep my head straight some days. Where am I going? What am I doing?" The challenge that arises for administrators and literacy specialists is to set clear goals and then ensure that the day-to-day responsibilities match those goals, without spreading the resources so thin that nothing is accomplished.

One of the unique challenges faced by literacy specialists at the elementary level is that their co-teachers, elementary educators, have had quite a lot of training and experience teaching reading and writing. Some elementary educators may believe that they know enough about teaching literacy, but just need a second set of hands. Others may believe that the methods they have been using for twenty years are good enough, and don't see a reason to change. A few may even voice their feelings as, "Who is this so-called specialist who is going to come into my room and show me how it's done?" In these situations, the literacy specialist has to confidently yet carefully establish her credibility. If, instead, the specialist crumbles in the face of resistance, students will pay the price. Reading specialist Emily Kendig advises her colleagues who are new to co-teaching: "Don't be afraid to be the specialist—you are an expert in reading! You have extra training and classes, and great ideas to bring to the table. My co-teachers have learned a lot of strategies from me, and in return I have learned a lot from them" (personal communication, 2010).

Essential for Success

Literacy specialists must be devoutly intentional in choosing strategies to incorporate into co-taught lessons. Achievement gains in reading and writing are most likely to occur when literacy specialists intentionally incorporate research-based practices (L'Allier, Elish-Piper, and Bean, 2010). Specialists cannot shy away from their expertise and knowledge; instead they must infuse it into the lessons at every opportunity. A visiting principal who observes a planning session or a lesson should be able to determine which teacher is the literacy specialist by virtue of the expertise she is contributing. It is important to remember that co-teaching is not about cloning—both teachers should not look exactly alike. Instead, co-teaching is about honoring the unique gifts that both teachers bring to their students.

> *Literacy specialists must be devoutly intentional in choosing strategies to incorporate into co-taught lessons.*

Partners must have time to collaboratively assess student progress in reading and writing. Detailed analysis to detect error patterns, gaps in understanding, and

> *It is important to remember that co-teaching is not about cloning—both teachers should not look exactly alike.*

responses to intervention will be most effective when both teachers can share their insights. The specialist is likely to have a thorough understanding of standardized test scores, whereas the classroom teacher will have valuable information about how a student is performing in the small, informal literacy moments that occur throughout the day. The classroom teacher is also more likely to have information about a student's home environment and the levels of literacy support that can be expected at home. By gathering as much information as possible, the co-teachers can utilize the data to design focused, individualized interventions. Time spent together in this endeavor will make a major impact on student outcomes.

TO SUM UP

- The co-teaching models used by a literacy specialist will depend, in part, on the school's approach to literacy. If small-group instruction is common, the Skill Groups Model will work well. If whole-class instruction is the norm, then the specialist will be likely to use the Complementary and Speak and Add models.

- Literacy specialists bring specific expertise to the classroom. While classroom teachers have general knowledge and experience in this arena, it is still important for the literacy specialist to assert her ideas and strategies when planning for co-taught lessons.

DISCUSSION QUESTIONS

- What unique challenges might a literacy specialist face when co-teaching?
- Which co-teaching model would you choose for a general education/ literacy specialist partnership? Why?
- How might a literacy specialist's expertise manifest itself in a co-taught language arts lesson? In a co-taught math, science, or history lesson?

CHAPTER 20

Co-Teaching with an ELL Specialist

Ms. Springer is preparing her classroom for the first day of school. She has always enjoyed the process of making name plates for each student desk, studying student photos as she tries to memorize the names. She knows how essential her relationship with each individual student will be to that child's success in her classroom. She carefully prints each name:

Josh, Jawid, Marisa, Tarik, Aaron, Aleese, Ben, Yong Sun, Rachel, Tonya, Jennifer, Faheema, Steven, Taelor, Amy, Bobby, Aandaleeb, Abbey, Jordan, Ryouko, Adolfo, Michelle

As Ms. Springer finishes the name plates, she reflects on how relieved she is to be co-teaching this year with an ELL teacher.

The National Center for Education Statistics, a branch of the U.S. Department of Education, reports that in 2008, 11 percent of the K–12 population in the United States was limited in English proficiency. Some states have ESL (English as a Second Language) populations as high as 25 percent. With numbers expected to grow, the need for classroom support is more urgent than ever.

Co-teaching is a sensible solution to this growing need. Benefits abound for English Language Learners. The co-teaching ELL specialist brings the expertise needed to make appropriate accommodations to the general education curriculum. In sharing her expertise, she models for the classroom teacher, in essence providing on-the-job training. The classroom teacher can then continue providing many of these strategies and accommodations throughout the school day, working constantly toward closing the achievement gap for ELL students. In addition to benefiting the ELL students, many of the strategies employed will benefit students who struggle in other ways.

ESL or ELL? What's the Difference?

In *Classroom Instruction That Works for English Language Learners*, Jane Hill and Kathleen Flynn (2006) define the terms ESL and ELL in light of program delivery. Hill and Flynn use the term "ESL (English as a Second Language)" to describe programs that provide specialized services, pull-out, and instruction from a trained teacher. The term "ELL (English Language Learner)" is used to describe services being provided in general education classrooms. Teachers try to accommodate for students with limited English proficiency in ways that make the curriculum more accessible.

Andrea Honigsfeld and Maria Dove, authors of *Collaboration and Co-Teaching: Strategies for English Learners*, advocate the use of the term English Learner (EL) over Limited English Proficiency (LEP) because it avoids placing emphasis on the deficiency (2010). By focusing on the process of acquiring new language, teachers shift to a capacity driven approach.

Best Models

The Duet Model is the most effective approach for co-teaching with an ELL specialist. By maintaining a constant presence and fully sharing responsibility for all phases of the instructional cycle, an ELL specialist can make a dramatic difference in the education of language learners. Some districts have recognized the benefits of the Duet Model and have allocated the staffing resources to make this happen.

> *By maintaining a constant presence and fully sharing responsibility for all phases of the instructional cycle, an ELL specialist can make a dramatic difference in the education of language learners.*

Jefferson County Public Schools in Colorado is moving toward a more inclusive model for their ELL services. Specialists are narrowing the number of classrooms in which they provide services by cluster grouping students who are English Language Learners. Instead of spreading themselves across six or more classrooms in an elementary building, specialists are creating schedules that allow them to focus their efforts on three or four classrooms. This frees the specialists to work with a few classrooms in more intensive ways—engaging in comprehensive planning with the classroom teachers, modeling instructional strategies in different content areas, and collaboratively shaping the formative and summative assessments.

Mary Weber, an ELL specialist with Jefferson County, recognizes the benefits of the Duet Model, observing: "Students need to be able to comprehend and participate in all classroom experiences. It is our responsibility to enable them to participate. As the ESL teacher, I need to model and co-teach so that students have access to the curriculum and so that classroom teachers can use these techniques with their students. When planning time allows, the Duet Model is the most effective way to accomplish this" (personal communication, 2010).

The third-grade lesson overview shown in Table 20.1 depicts the ideas generated in co-planning for an integrated, duet lesson. The partners brought different but compatible perspectives to the content objectives, generating ideas that enhance instruction for targeted

TABLE 20.1: Co-Taught Lesson with a ELL Specialist

Third Grade: Science Unit—Life Cycles, Lesson on Butterfly Stages Ideas for Core Vocabulary	
MR. WHITESELL—CLASSROOM TEACHER	MRS. EMMANUEL—ELL SPECIALIST
Prediction activity Video on butterflies Chart of life cycle, labeled with vocabulary Definition review Nonfiction and fiction selections (various reading levels) about butterflies for independent and guided reading	Visual images for each vocabulary word Photos of butterflies found in other countries, with corresponding world map Mix-and-match activity for images and vocabulary words Sentence frames "The first stage in the life cycle of the butterfly is _____." Sentence starters with picture cues for Think-Pair-Share

students, as well as others. After generating the ideas, the teachers shared the instructional leading, shifting smoothly back and forth when appropriate. Both teachers monitored student comprehension carefully, making immediate adjustments or jotting down notes to discuss when co-planning the next day's lesson.

For most districts, economic factors limit the amount of time that ELL teachers can spend planning, implementing, and assessing instruction with their general education colleagues. With limited time, ELL teachers generally find the most effective co-teaching models to be the Speak and Add, Learning Style, and the Adapting models, which encourage the specialist to make on-the-spot changes or additions to the lesson, without a lot of co-planning. Often the specialist will carry a tool kit from class to class, filled with simple items that apply to many lessons. Popular tool kit items include:

- Picture schedules
- Highlighters and highlighter tape
- Thesaurus
- Picture cards
- Colored pencils
- Blank sentence strips
- Picture dictionary
- Discussion chips⊕
- Colored acetate strips

When an ELL teacher uses the Speak and Add Model, her contributions are likely to be much more frequent than when other specialists use this model. In any mini-lecture that a classroom teacher presents, there will be many instances when students with limited English proficiency will need information restated or clarified. Similarly, there will be many times when a visual or tactile image will make the information more easily accessible. The classroom teacher will want to be relaxed and flexible about these frequent additions, seeing them as enrichments rather than interruptions.

⊕ See Appendix A

Challenges

One of the unique challenges for co-teaching a class that includes several ELL students is the language barrier. This challenge increases exponentially when there are multiple languages present in the room. Teachers can be intimidated and frustrated by their inability to communicate effectively with students and parents. Even the most dedicated teacher may hesitate to take on this challenge willingly.

Cultural differences may also be seen as enough of a challenge to deter teachers from accepting a co-teaching role. For example, cultures can vary in the type of engagement and responsiveness they encourage. In the United States, during a conventional classroom lecture teachers typically expect students to think silently and raise their hands with a correct answer. However, some cultures encourage communal problem solving and rapport-talk (Gay, 2000). When students raised in this way are members of a class, there may be an increase in noise, talking out of turn, and interrupting. These behaviors can be viewed as rude and disruptive and some teachers may try to eliminate them. However, in a co-taught ELL classroom, teachers will need to know background information about their students' cultures in order to interpret learning behaviors correctly, and be open to changing some of their tried-and-true methods of classroom management and instruction.

A less obvious but significant problem occurs as students achieve greater and greater success with the English language. Many students are able to communicate with enough verbal fluency to get their meaning across to peers and teachers. However, closer examination may show that underlying language structures and academic vocabulary are weak. Similarly, students may develop adequate decoding skills and appear to be on or near grade level in reading, but have weak comprehension and retelling skills. These surface level behaviors may lead the classroom teacher to believe that accommodations are no longer necessary. The ELL specialist may find herself in the role of having to convince her partner that they still need to do the extra work—creating and implementing the accommodations and supports to help ELL students achieve a deeper and more lasting success.

Essential for Success

A teacher who is flexible, embraces cultural diversity, and is truly interested in learning about other cultures will be most successful at co-teaching a classroom with a cluster of English learners. These traits will enhance his relationships with these students, a key first step. When ELL students join a class, they are likely to feel high anxiety (Haynes, 2007). Anxiety can impede language processing and learning, resulting in slower progress. A teacher can make an enormous difference in alleviating some of the culture shock and anxiety by greeting students with a smile, using body language to supplement verbal messages, playing native music in the classroom, and displaying pictures from the students' home countries. As the teacher gets to know individual students, he will gather valuable information about their backgrounds, thus allowing him to tap into their schema when teaching.

> *A teacher who is flexible, embraces cultural diversity, and is truly interested in learning about other cultures will be most successful at co-teaching a classroom with a cluster of English learners.*

Larry Ferlazzo, ELL teacher and author, reminds us that "English language learners often have very different background knowledge than what native speakers bring to class. By learning about students' lives, educators can more effectively connect those experiences with new classroom content" (2010).

These traits—flexibility, interest in other cultures—will also enable the teacher to facilitate successful peer interactions. In a co-taught class for ELL students, cooperative group work and peer interaction will be essential for success. To ensure effective group work, co-teaching partners will want to spend some time at the beginning of the year helping students to get to know each other. In addition, it will be worthwhile to teach specific skills for group work—skills such as turn taking, clarifying, leading, and recording. When group work is assigned, co-teaching partners will want to provide specific directions that ensure everyone's participation. Cooperative learning structures, such as Numbered Heads Together or Think-Pair-Timed Share (Kagan and Kagan, 2008) have been proven effective for heterogeneous groups of students.

In addition to cooperative learning, co-teachers will want to incorporate a significant amount of visual, tactile, and kinesthetic teaching strategies. While these strategies are helpful to many students, they are especially crucial to ELL students. For example, a traditional auditory lecture, because it is dependent on language knowledge, will pass right over the heads of many ELL students, leaving them frustrated and lost. Conversely, a lecture that is supported by descriptive photos, visual time lines, maps, props, manipulatives, gestures, and demonstrations will make much more sense. The ELL specialist's expertise will make it easy for the partners to generate a variety of simple ideas for multimodality instruction.

TO SUM UP

- The Duet Model is ideal for co-teaching with an ELL specialist. It allows for constant infusion of the specialist's expertise with language acquisition. When time constraints make this impossible, specialists find that the Speak and Add, Learning Style, and Adapting models work well.

- When ELL specialists use the Speak and Add Model for co-teaching, it will be much more intensive than with other specialists. Partners should discuss ways to plan flexibly for a lot of back-and-forth between adults, so that students and adults are comfortable.

DISCUSSION QUESTIONS

- What teacher attributes might be best for co-teaching with an ELL specialist?

- Compare the various models suggested for co-teaching with an ELL specialist. Which would you choose? Why?

- Picture a co-taught class where 25 percent of students are English Language Learners. During a Speak and Add Model, what might the ELL teacher be doing?

PART FOUR

WRAPPING IT UP

CHAPTER 21

Conclusion: Evolving Partnerships

Recently a small toy store in my hometown held a big clearance sale. I was there, wandering the aisles, looking for intriguing items that might add some novelty to my teaching. Halfway down one aisle was a very small boy, only tall enough to see into the baskets of toys on the lowest shelf. His mother had plopped down on the floor beside him and was holding a plastic kaleidoscope to his eye. His chubby hands were not yet dexterous enough to hold it in place and turn the end, so she was helping him with the task. As I watched, she gradually released her hold on the kaleidoscope and let him twist it all by himself. His joy was contagious! After a few attempts it was working—perhaps not with the smoothness his mother might have offered, but better and better with passing time.

Successful co-teaching takes time as well. True partnerships develop as trust builds, as the ups and downs are shared, as skills emerge. During the first year of working together, most co-teachers find that they are getting to know each other's teaching styles and philosophies, working out the kinks of shared responsibilities, and recognizing each other's talents. In the second year, co-teachers develop fluidity, an ease of interaction. This frees teachers from spending their talk time on less consequential details and allows them to focus on quality instruction. Reflections are more powerful, more honest, and lead to better instructional decisions. By the third year, with a strong foundation laid, co-teachers work smoothly and smartly together. They easily share responsibilities, shift plans responsively, and shape instruction—all while making it look almost effortless. Time together has allowed them to create a powerful partnership for students.

Some co-teaching teams find their flow much more quickly, while others move more slowly. For the sake of our students, effective co-teaching must be

For the sake of our students, effective co-teaching must be fast-tracked.

fast-tracked. We cannot afford to underutilize a specialist in a co-taught class, nor can we afford to allow poor co-teaching to interfere with good teaching. The ideas and tools presented in this book have been proven to assist educators in moving their co-teaching efforts forward. It is my sincerest hope that they will help you, too.

Instructional Strategies for Co-Taught Classrooms

Bloom's Connection Puzzles	Discussion Chips	Temple Strategy
Board Relay	Group Graffiti	Text Messaging Summary
Brain Bookmarks	Highlighter Tape	The Answer Is ...
Challenge Authority Cards	Multiple Perspective Glasses	The Back of a Napkin
Character Layers	Pen the Tale	Virtual Tug-of-War Debate
Colored Acetate Strips	RAFTs	Webquest
Connection Collection	Spelling Word Relay Teams	Work Masks
Deal or No Deal	Symbolic Summary	You Lose Bingo

Bloom's Connection Puzzles

Capitalizing on the human compulsion to fill in missing pieces, this strategy utilizes jigsaw puzzle pieces to encourage students to make higher-level connections. It incorporates all four sensory modalities in a low-prep, cross-content activity.

How to . . .

1. Copy the Bloom's Connection Puzzle reproducible onto magnetic paper (available from office supply stores) or card stock. Cut the

jigsaw pieces apart. If using card stock, adhere a small magnet to the back of each puzzle piece.

2. Stick the magnets to a magnetic white board, showing the correct hierarchy, and explain Bloom's Taxonomy to the students.

3. Disassemble the puzzle, leaving the pieces scattered on the board. Tell the students that their task is to assemble the puzzle pieces by the end of the lesson (or unit.) In order to put a piece into place, a student must make a connection at that level of the taxonomy. For example, during a lesson on the ancient Egyptian ruler Thutmose IV, students made the following connections. As each piece was put into place, a few key words were written on the board next to it.

   - Creating—"Machines could be invented that automatically lay bricks for the temples to speed up the building process. Kind of like the assembly plants for cars."

   - Evaluating—"If Thutmose had not been so vain and extravagant in his building projects, less people would have been employed. More people would have starved. So maybe he was a good ruler."

   - Analyzing—"Maybe Thutmose IV was like FDR. We learned about him and the Civilian Conservation Corp. He helped society by putting them to work."

   - Applying—"My church youth group raises money to buy animals through the Heifer Project. They say that giving someone an animal provides them with a job and a future, rather than just giving them food."

   - Understanding—"For someone in charge, Thutmose didn't accomplish a lot. Mostly he just built stuff. My dad says that our current president isn't accomplishing much either."

   - Remembering—"I saw something about those Egyptian monuments on the History Channel a few months ago."

4. As students make connections, allow them to come up and put the related puzzle pieces in place. Write a few descriptive words next to each piece to capture the connection.

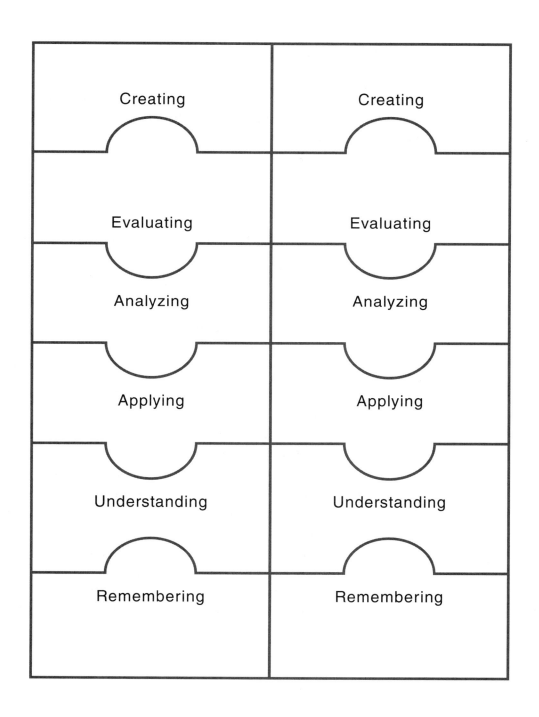

Board Relay

Board Relay is an energizing activity that uses inconsequential competition to engage students in completing an assigned task. It can be used across grade levels and content areas, with very little preparation on the part of the teacher.

How to . . .

1. Divide the class into four relay teams. Team membership should be heterogeneous.

2. Review the rules of Board Relay with the students:

    -   No running.

    -   No shouting out answers.

    -   Marker or chalk must be placed on the ledge after each turn.

    -   Winners will be determined based on accuracy as well as speed.

3. Divide the board into four sections and place chalk or a marker on the ledge beneath each section.

4. Determine the task for Board Relay. For example, students might be required to list elements or examples of the concept just taught, compose a sentence using an assigned vocabulary word, skip-count by fives to fifty, and so on.

5. Explain to students that they will each take a turn in completing the task, as in a relay. Depending on the assignment, clarify for students how much should be done in each turn. For example, in skip counting by fives, each student would list the next number in the sequence. Students will most likely have multiple turns before the round is over.

6. Explain that finish times will be kept for each team, but that finishing first does not mean winning—accuracy is more important.

7. Determine and convey a scoring system. For example, finishing first is worth 100 points, second 90 points, third 80 points, and fourth 70 points, but for every error the team loses 15 points.

8. Start the Board Relay. As necessary, remind students of the rules.

9. Mark the finishing order of each team on the board. When the last team has completed the task, engage the whole group in reviewing the work of each team for accuracy.

10. Note total scores for each team and try again with a new task!

Variations . . .

*   Board Relays can be done in partners, so that no student is left on his own to complete a step of the task. Partners should be assigned by the teacher with the purpose of pairing a more able student with a student in need of support.

*   Relay teams can be given thirty seconds before the start to strategize about their approach to the task. This will allow struggling students to hear ideas from their peers.

*   If boards are not available, place four sheets of chart paper on the wall, one per team.

*   Seated Relay is a variation that reduces the physical movement in the room. For Seated Relay you will need one small whiteboard and marker per team. The student in the first position of the relay writes on the white board while seated at her desk, and then passes it back to the next student.

Brain Bookmarks

Metacognition, the act of thinking about thinking, is an important skill for students. When a student is aware of her attention to a task and the many ways her brain might approach the task, she can gain more control over the process. However, the concept of metacognition is very abstract and can be difficult for some students to grasp. This is especially true during independent activities, such as silent reading, in which a teacher is not guiding the thinking process. Brain Bookmarks provide the necessary cues for students to develop awareness of metacognition.

How to . . .

1. Provide each student with a Brain Bookmark cut out from the reproducible.

2. Explain to students that medical imaging technology has shown that areas of the brain light up with electrical impulses when they are being used. (Brief video clips of this can be found on the Internet and shown for emphasis.)

3. Further explain that some researchers believe that we can improve our own brain function by being aware of our thought processes. This is called metacognition or "thinking about thinking."

4. Point out the different metacognitive prompts on the Brain Bookmark and explain as necessary.

5. Show students how they can use a yellow highlighter to highlight a section on their Brain Bookmarks that corresponds to their thinking. The goal is to eventually highlight all of the metacognition prompts.

6. Encourage students to glance at their bookmark before, during, and after they read.

Variation . . .

- Suggest that students write short sentences on the back of the Brain Bookmark that describe their thinking.

Brain Bookmark

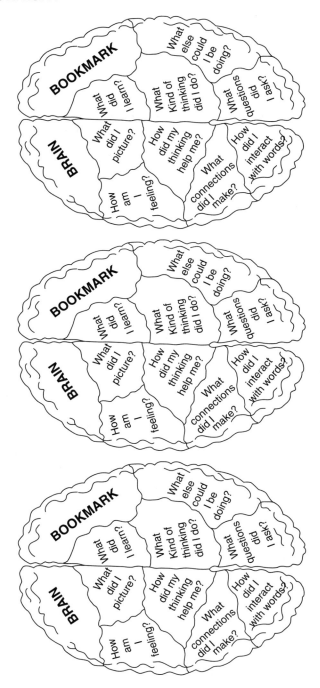

Challenge Authority Cards

The process of challenging authority involves several higher order thinking skills. Often, this type of critical dialogue is discouraged in classrooms, as many teachers are most comfortable with compliant students. The Challenge Authority Card strategy is a simple, make-ahead tool that can spark engaging discourse in a structured manner. Especially intriguing for students who are ready for higher level thinking, the cards are an easy way to address the needs of gifted students within the context of a heterogeneous class.

How to . . .

1. Copy the Challenge Authority Cards reproducible. Cut the cards apart. If desired, laminate each card for durability.

2. At the beginning of a lesson, distribute the cards to individual students who are ready for an intellectual challenge.

3. Explain to the whole class that some students have been given a task to do during the lesson. On future days other students will also have the chance to try the tasks.

4. As the lesson progresses, encourage students with Challenge Authority Cards to look for opportunities to follow through on their tasks.

Challenge Authority Cards

Prepare a false answer to one of the questions and be prepared to try to convince others that you are correct.

Listen for a point that the teacher makes that you think you could debate. Debate the teacher, using supportive examples or evidence to prove your point.

Question the text. Did the textbook authors make any errors? Use any poor examples? Have a biased perspective? Leave out something essential?

How could you "fix" this experiment/game/situation (cheat) so that the outcome would be different?

Character Layers

Character Layers use a readily available scrap material to emphasize concepts that have layers or depth to them. Students can write and draw on the laminate layers with water-based markers, making them a visual and tactile instructional material.

How to . . .

1. Collect leftover scraps of laminate. (Clear plastic report covers, available from office supply stores, work equally well.)

2. Cut the laminate into strips approximately three-by-eight inches in size.

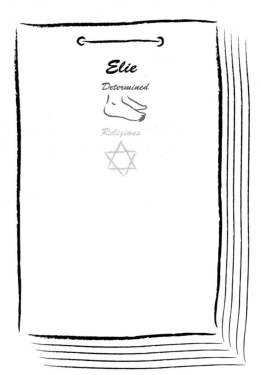

Figure A.1:

3. Stack six strips directly on top of each other and staple them together at one of the narrow ends.

4. Provide each student with one set of strips and a water-based wipe-off marker.

5. Assign a character to each student. If there are several characters being studied, assign the more complicated characters to the students most ready for a challenge.

6. Direct the students to write their character's name on the first strip. On each successive strip, they are to write a character trait of that individual, and draw a simple, symbolic representation of that trait. The words and drawings should progress from top to bottom (see Figure A.1). For example, if considering Elie Wiesel from *Night*, a student might write the word "determined" and draw marching feet. On the next strip, the student might write "religious" and draw a Star of David.

7. After students have designed their layers, call each student up to the overhead projector or document camera. The student begins by showing the last strip first, progressively adding each layer, until all that is left to be revealed is the character's name. Other students try to guess the character based on the descriptions provided.

Variations . . .

*   Use layers to show steps in a process that build upon each other, such as the steps in photosynthesis or the layers of the earth. Laminate layers can also be used for concepts that have a hierarchy, such as the branches of government, the food web, or superlatives.

*   Cut six-by-six-inch pieces of laminate for teaching students about multiple line graphs. Students can draw a different line on each layer and see how they intersect with each other.

Colored Acetate Strips

Colored Acetate Strips fit over a text page to highlight two or three lines of text at a time. As students read, they slide the strip down the page to continually highlight the lines being read. This strategy is effective for improving visual attention and reading fluency.

How to . . .

1. Obtain several Colored Glide Bind Report Covers (available from office supply stores.) Cut the covers into strips that are wide enough to cover three lines of text in a commonly used book. Be sure that the strips include the fold from the edge of the report cover so that it can wrap around the page.

2. Direct students to place the colored acetate strips over their book page, one half on the back of the page, one half on the front.

3. Model for the students how to fluidly slide the strip down the page as they read, highlighting a few lines of text at a time.

4. Explain to students that the strip will also help to save their place if they stop for a moment to discuss a feature of the text.

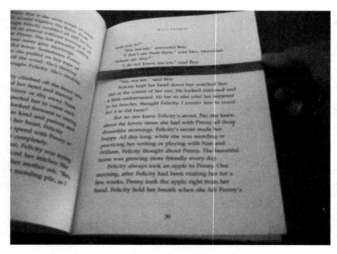

Figure A.2: Colored Acetate Strips

5. Allow students to sample the different colors to determine which one they prefer.

Connection Collection

To encourage students to make connections between prior knowledge and new learning, set up a Connection Collection board in the classroom. The board will highlight a theme or concept from the unit, and whenever a student makes a connection to the theme it is added to the board.

How to . . .

1. Find a place in the room that can be dedicated to your Connection Collection. This might be a section of your whiteboard, a bulletin board, or a chart hung on a wall. Label it "Connection Collection."

2. Explain to students that they will be recording any connections that are made between their prior knowledge and new learning.

3. Model and lead a connection activity. For example, in a math class the concept being studied might be polygons. Write this heading on the board and then suggest a connection, such as "the newspaper is shaped like a polygon." Ask students for ideas they have.

4. Encourage them to move to higher level examples such as "knowledge of polygons can help figure out the volume of a box."

5. Throughout the week, encourage students to share connections as they think of them. Have the students add the ideas to the board.

Variations . . .

- Take a photo of the Connection Collection before removing it and upload it to your class website.

- Have students copy the connections into their subject-area notebooks.

Deal or No Deal

This popular game show serves as an effective hook for student attention. Student contestants choose a briefcase that contains an unknown element. When the element is revealed, students use it to practice vocabulary in novel contexts. The cases contain a variety of contexts in which students can practice vocabulary application.

How to . . .

1. Gather a dozen or more three-by-five-inch index cards. Fold them in half to form a briefcase shape that measures three by two-and-a-half inches, and stick them closed with a bit of sticky tack.

2. Number the outside of the cases. Inside each case, write an occupation that your students might be familiar with. These could include firefighter, doctor, teacher, computer specialist, game designer, baseball player, and truck driver.

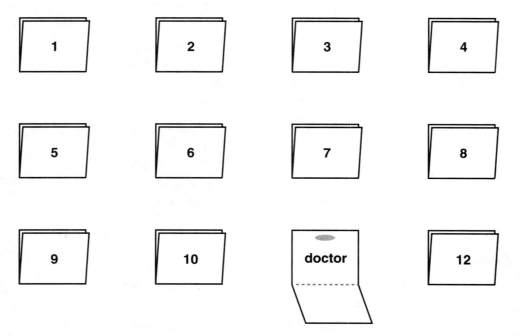

Figure A.3:

3. Hang the cases on a wall or bulletin board where students can access them.

4. When introducing a new vocabulary word to students, share the definition and discuss the meaning. Explain to students that it is important to know how to use words in contexts other than school.

5. Point out the cases and ask if they have seen a television show that has a similar array of briefcases (*Deal or No Deal*). Explain that, instead of money, these cases contain jobs where people can earn money. Students are to imagine how someone who has that job might use the new vocabulary word in his or her work.

6. Select a student to be the first contestant, open the suitcase of his choice, and read aloud the job he has won.

7. Direct students to talk with a peer and develop a sentence that uses the new word in the chosen occupation. If necessary, provide an example. If the vocabulary word was "regulate" and the occupation selected is firefighter, an example might be "Firefighters have to regulate campfires in drought-stricken areas."

Variations . . .

- Replace the occupations with locations, names of famous people, or with a variety of hobbies. Ask students to apply vocabulary words in these other contexts.

- Place a number in each case and use the numbers for random pairing of students, selection of a problem to answer, or development of math stories.

Discussion Chips

Small-group participation skyrockets when students have strategic tools to help them. In this visual/tactile strategy, students are provided with poker chips covered with graphic cues related to a variety of discussion strategies. Students are encouraged to toss a relevant poker chip into a container when they have something to say. The similarity to playing poker adds a game-like quality that enhances student participation.

How to . . .

1. Make copies of the Discussion Chip reproducible and cut out the icons. If desired, adhere each one to the top of a poker chip. Decide which chips are relevant to the topic to be discussed.

2. Ask students if they have ever played poker. Describe how poker players must choose to participate by calling "I'm in" and tossing poker chips into the middle of the table. Share phrases such as "get your head in the game" or "I'm really into skateboarding."

3. Distribute a set of relevant chips to each student.

4. Discuss the icons and what they might represent in a discussion about your content.

5. Explain to students that when they are ready to participate in the discussion, they are to toss in a poker chip that represents the comment or question they would like to make. For example, if a student wants to piggyback on another student's insight, he would toss in the "pig" poker chip.

6. Arrange students into small discussion groups and provide each group with a paper plate or small container. Direct students to sit in a circle and place the container in the center.

7. Monitor students as they engage in discussion. If you notice students who have not put in a poker chip, ask them to look at the pictures on the chips to help them think of something to add.

8. If desired, have students pause halfway through the discussion period and reflect on how "in the game" they are.

Discussion Chips

predicting

piggybacking

summarizing

feelings

connections

question

vocabulary

cause/effect

inference

a-ha moment

challenge

restate

Group Graffiti

Group Graffiti is a quick, creative way to awaken prior knowledge or reinforce new learning. Like graffiti (also known as tagging), thoughts or ideas are expressed in simple but bold artistic messages. The visual display is an appealing alternative to other brainstorming or K-W-L activities.

How to . . .

1. Cut two eight-foot lengths of white butcher paper.

2. Explain to students that they will be "tagging" or making graffiti about the lesson topic on the butcher paper. Remind students that graffiti usually consists of simple visual images or words, often symbolic. Add that they will be working on the floor so that the different plane will spark their creativity.

3. Have students grab a marker from their desk, backpack, or supply bin.

4. Ask students to quickly arrange the desks so that there are two large open floor areas, and then place the paper on the floor.

5. Divide the class into two groups and have students sit around the edges of the paper.

6. Write the topic (one to three words) in large print in the middle of the butcher paper.

7. Direct students to use their markers to quickly tag the paper with anything they can think of about the topic. For example, if the topic is "meteors," students might write words such as "space, moving, large, hard, fall to earth" or draw symbols representing planets, earth, movement, speed, gravity, danger, orbits, or showers.

8. After a few minutes, stop the students. Have the two groups face each other, holding their graffiti poster for the others to see. Facilitate discussion about the words and symbols that came to mind for the topic.

Highlighter Tape

A removable alternative to highlighter pens for all kinds of texts, Highlighter Tape sticks securely, yet removes easily and is reusable. This tool is a wonderful adaptation for students who need the extra focus of highlighting but can't write in the text.

How to . . .

1. Obtain Highlighter Tape from an office supply store or website.

2. Laminate thirty index cards for durability.

3. Place six or eight short strips of highlighter tape on each card. One end of each strip should have a tab folded under to make it easy to peel off. If available, use two different colors of tape so that you can choose to ask students to color code items.

4. Pass out the cards at the beginning of a text activity. Direct students to highlight specific words related to your lesson. For example, students might be directed to highlight important dates, adjectives, examples of alliteration, or directions.

5. At the end of the lesson, ask students to place the tape back on the cards before handing them in.

Variations . . .

- Send Highlighter Tape cards home with students to use when they are reading or studying. Direct them to highlight words or concepts that are confusing so that they can review them in class the following day.

Multiple Perspective Glasses

One way to add depth in almost any content area is to encourage students to view the topic from a perspective other than their own. Classroom discussion may bring in the perspective of their peers or teachers, but moving beyond the classroom walls can develop greater depth of understanding. A simple way to accomplish this is through Multiple Perspective Glasses. The props—mirrored sunglasses—add a novel element to liven the discussion.

How to . . .

1. Collect several old sunglasses or purchase inexpensive ones at a party or novelty supply store.

2. Using a water-based transparency marker, write the name of a well known individual on each pair of lenses. Names might include celebrities, politicians, historical figures, or athletes. Names might also stem from your content. For example, in a lesson on the American Revolution, the glasses might include George Washington, a merchant, a military horse, a British soldier, Martin Luther King, Jr., Oprah Winfrey, and Justin Bieber.

3. Place the sunglasses in a container.

4. Ask students to form small groups, and have one student in each group reach into the container and grab a pair of sunglasses.

5. Direct groups to discuss the topic from the perspective of the person they drew.

6. After a few minutes, ask groups to share their insights with the whole class.

7. Wipe off the lenses with a damp tissue and choose new names for new content.

Variation . . .

- Increase the challenge by choosing inanimate objects to write on the lenses. For example, in a lesson on triangles, students might consider the perspective of an acute angle, a vertex, a line, or a circle.

Pen the Tale

A variation on the popular RAFT approach for differentiation, Pen the Tale is a strategy for expanding students' ideas for writing topics. Students randomly select a role, and then purposefully choose from a list of formats and actions. The process gives students the opportunity to explore new ideas and develop a creative writing piece.

How to . . .

1. Copy the Pen the Tale reproducible for each student. Enlarge one copy and place it on the board.

2. Provide each student with one colored restickable dot.

3. Ask the students if they are familiar with the popular party game, Pin the Tail on the Donkey. Draw comparisons, explaining that students will use the sticky dots instead of a tail to play Pen the Tale.

4. Select one student to help demonstrate. Ask him to close his eyes (or place a loose blindfold over his eyes).

5. Spin him twice and then aim him at the donkey. Direct him to stick his dot somewhere on the donkey chart.

6. Ask him to open his eyes to see what role he has selected. This will be the character closest to the dot.

7. Model how to choose an action the character will write about and a format for the writing.

8. Demonstrate once more before asking students to try it on their own papers.

9. After the students have selected all three components—role, action, format—direct them to list these in the idea section of their Writer's Notebooks.

10. Repeat until students have recorded several different writing ideas for future use.

Variations . . .

- Ask students to add characters to their donkeys whenever they think of them.

- Develop a Pen the Tale reproducible that has an alternate set of actions and formats to provide variety for students.

Pen the Tale

baby   dancer

spider

firefighter   quarterback

mother

teacher

child   astronaut

alien

rapper   pig

puppy

flower   clown   pirate

Action	Format
Eating ice cream	Story
Flying in a plane	Poem
Riding a horse	Song lyrics
Swimming in the ocean	Love letter
Playing a sport	Directions
Making cookies	Conversation
Hunting for treasure	News article
Singing in a contest	Interview
Losing a pet	Bulleted list
Going to a party	Advice column
Opening a gift	Thank you note
Saying goodbye	Non-fiction

RAFTs

The RAFT strategy, originally conceived by Nancy Vandevanter as part of the Montana Writing Project (Santa, 2004), uses writing or performance activities to enhance understanding of information. Instead of writing a traditional short answer or essay to show knowledge and understanding, the students demonstrate their understanding in a nontraditional format. This technique encourages creative thinking and motivates students to reflect in unusual ways about concepts they have learned.

How to . . .

1. Develop a table with a heading that is similar to the RAFT example below.

2. Begin with developing ideas for the Topic column, as this represents your learning objectives. You may choose just one topic for the entire column, or several topics. Next, complete the other three columns. Strive for one row that represents a higher level of complexity, two rows that represent grade-level complexity, and one row that has a simpler level of complexity. Explore the list of ideas on page 225.

3. Explain to students what each letter in RAFT represents.

   • R = Role of the writer: What is the writer's role? Options might include a reporter, observer, or object related to the content.

   • A = Audience: Who will be reading or receiving the writing? Options might include the teacher, people in the community, historical figures, or an object related to the content.

   • F = Format: What is the best way to present this information? Options might include a letter, an article, a poem, or an advertisement.

   • T = Topic: What do we want the student to know and demonstrate? What is the objective or standard?

4. Allow students to choose any row that appeals to them as a way to show their knowledge of the subject matter. If necessary, offer guidance to individual students so that they make a choice matching their readiness level.

Example: Earth Science RAFT

R	A	F	T
ROLE	AUDIENCE	FORMAT	TOPIC
P. Diddy	California Legislature	Rap or poem	Describe the theory of Plate Tectonics
Broadcaster	The general public	News report	Compare and contrast the three types of plate boundaries
Sixth-grade student	Wegener's critics	Perform a skit with one other person	Compare and contrast plate tectonics with continental drift
Steve Jobs	MAC World Convention	Design a home page that includes links	Evidence supporting the development of the theory of plate tectonics from previous theories
Wegener	Wilson or Hess	Thank-you note	A note defending his point of view
Wegener	Wegener's sister	Two-sided postcard	Describe or draw the evidence for continental drift

RAFT Ideas

ROLE	AUDIENCE	FORMAT	TOPIC
writer	self	journal	expected
artist	peer group	editorial	content
character	government	brochure/	knowledge or
scientist	parents	booklet	skill
adventurer	fictional	interview	issue relevant to
inventor	character(s)	video	the text or time
juror	committee	song lyric	period
judge	jury	cartoon	topic of personal
historian	judge	game	interest or
reporter	activists	primary	concern for the
rebel	immortality	document	role or audience
therapist	animals or	critique	topic related to
journalist	objects	biographical	an essential
food item	weather	sketch	question
plant	ocean	newspaper	
inanimate object	tree	article	
candidate	pen	complaint	
new mother	cell phone	advice column	
superhero	food	text message	
heart	vehicle	horoscope	
water	pillow	thank-you note	
		speech	
		rap or song	
		closing	
		argument	

Spelling Word Relay Teams

Minor competition motivates many students to practice mundane learning tasks. In Spelling Word Relay Teams, students race their peers to spell out new spelling words for the week. The kinesthetic input causes the release of endorphins, helpful for neural processing and retention. This strategy can be used by classroom teachers with access to a large running space, or by the physical education teacher.

How to . . .

1. Obtain three hundred large paper or plastic drink cups. Place a single cup upside down on a desk. Using a marker, write the letter A on the front and back of the cup. Continue through the alphabet, making twelve of each letter. Twelve sets will allow you to work with four to six relay teams (depending on how frequently a letter is used in a word, for example, *believe*).

2. Place the cups on the floor at one end of the running space, and set up the relay teams at the opposite end.

3. Explain to students that you will call out a word from their current spelling list. On "Go" the first student on each team is to run down, retrieve a cup with the first letter, and bring it back to their team. Immediately, the second student runs to get the second letter. The team continues until they have completed spelling the word. Whichever team finishes first and correctly wins the round.

4. Continue playing for as many rounds as desired.

5. For added challenge, tell students that you will occasionally surprise them with a word from a previous spelling list.

6. Use this strategy for practicing math facts by adding numbers to the other sides of the cups.

Symbolic Summary

Nonlinguistic representations can be a powerful memory enhancer for students. The Symbolic Summary strategy encourages students to augment their notes with quick, symbolic representations of their learning.

How to . . .

1. Determine how many key concepts (four, six, or eight) you want to reinforce with the use of the Symbolic Summary.

2. Provide students with a loose sheet of plain white paper and ask them to fold the paper into fourths, sixths, or eighths.

3. After the first concept has been taught, tell the students that they will have one minute to draw a quick picture in the first space on their paper. The picture is to represent what they just learned, without using any words. Explain that the drawings should be simple, such as icons, logos, or symbols, rather than extremely detailed.

4. When fifty seconds have passed, give students a ten-second countdown. Then ask students to turn and share their drawing with a peer. If desired, solicit one or two students to share with the class.

5. Continue with each key concept, filling the paper with symbolic drawings. Have students store the paper in their notebooks for later review.

Temple Strategy

Understanding main idea and supporting detail requires students to recognize the relationship between components or ideas. There is usually a hierarchy, in which one idea sits over, or encompasses, the other ideas. The Temple Strategy reinforces this understanding by using a Greek temple as a visual metaphor.

How to . . .

1. Cut craft foam or construction paper into the temple shapes as shown in the Temple Strategy reproducible. The roof should be green, the pillars yellow, and the thought cloud white. Each student can have his or her own set, or you may have them work in partners and share a set.

2. Cut strips of plain paper, approximately one-by-four inches, for students to write on.

3. Show students a photo of a Greek temple and explain that it was a place where learned men went to exchange important ideas under one roof. Make a connection between this and main idea and supporting details in a piece of text—that several ideas (the pillars) fall under one main idea (the roof).

4. Model this concept with a set of words such as "happy, sad, emotions, angry." Begin by writing each word on a strip of paper, and then adhere each word to the appropriate temple piece.

5. After practicing with single words, move to a short paragraph. Ask students to identify four ideas from the text that are important. Model how to decide which one encompasses the other three (this will usually come from the topic sentence.)

6. As students are ready, move to longer paragraphs and then multiple paragraph texts.

7. The thought cloud can be used for students who are ready to work with the more complex concept of theme. Explain that theme, like the cloud, may not be specifically expressed within the text, but is a universal concept such as "do unto others" or "interdependence of all living things."

Variation

- Students may use the Temple Strategy reproducible as a graphic organizer when planning a piece of their own writing.

Temple Strategy

Text Message Summary

Text Messaging is a popular communication shortcut very familiar to students. Teachers can use this interest to practice succinct summarization of curriculum content.

How to . . .

1. Copy the Text Message Cell Phone reproducible and distribute one to each student.

2. Direct students to write a text message summary of their learning in the screen area, as if they were texting to a friend. Encourage them to use some of the shortcuts and alternative spelling that they might normally use when texting.

3. When they have finished their text message, ask them to count up the number of characters used and record the total in the small box at the bottom of the screen.

4. Encourage students to share their summaries with the class. This can be done verbally, or the cell phones can be shown under a document camera.

5. After the first summary is shared, ask the student how many characters were used. Then survey the class to see if anyone thinks they were able to capture the main idea of the learning with fewer characters.

6. Continue sharing for an appropriate amount of time.

Variations . . .

- Use text messaging as an exit slip. Near the end of the class period, distribute the paper cell phones and direct students to write a text message describing one thing they learned in class, or one thing they still have questions about. Each student must hand in a cell phone as they exit class.

- Use Internet sites such as www.polleverywhere.com to do live polling with students. Students use their cell phones to text in a response to a question the teacher has designed in advance. The website is projected onto the screen and students can watch their text message responses being received in real time.

Text Message Cell Phone

The Answer Is . . .

This simple strategy promotes higher order thinking and can be used to activate prior knowledge or make connections. The Answer Is . . . can be used as a one-time activity or be made available for students to respond to during the course of a week or unit.

How to . . .

1. Cut a four-foot section of butcher paper or obtain a piece of chart paper.

2. Place the paper on the floor, surrounded by colored markers.

3. In the center of the paper write the phrase "The answer is . . . " followed by a single word. The word may be related to your content, or could be randomly selected. For example, in a geometry lesson, the word might be "square" or "jumping."

4. Direct students to generate questions that are answered by the chosen word, and write them on the paper. They can work individually or in pairs. Examples for "square" might include:

   - What do you call a rectangle having all four sides of equal length?

   - What shape is a box?

   - What kind of person does not break the rules?

   - What type of numbers are these: 1, 4, 9, 16, 25?

   - What kind of dance has a caller?

   - What shape is used in hopscotch?

   Examples for jumping might include

   - How do you wake up if your foot has fallen asleep?

   - What rhymes with pumping?

   - What are people doing when they are really excited?

   - What is the kid doing on the trampoline?

   - What is the frog doing?

5. Discuss student questions, highlighting the variety of thinking shown.

6. Hang the chart in a place that is accessible to students so that they can continue to generate questions throughout the week.

The Back of a Napkin

Many great ideas have been developed on the back of a napkin. Simple drawings can capture the essence of a concept in a unique way that may be more powerful than a paragraph of words. The Back of a Napkin strategy encourages students to capture their learning and ideas in a non-linguistic representation, using a readily available but unexpected medium.

How to . . .

1. Obtain a paper napkin for each student. (High quality is not important—often the cheaper napkins, like those found at fast-food restaurants and coffee shops, work best.)

2. Explain to students that many brilliant ideas and booming businesses have been developed on the back of a napkin. One company started this way is Southwest Airlines. (For details and additional examples, check out *The Back of a Napkin* by Dan Roam.)

   Direct students to capture their learning by drawing a simple design on their napkins. Words can be off-limits entirely or limited to a few. If desired, share an example, as shown in the figure. Students in an Algebra course had been taught the Golden Rule of Algebra ("Do unto one side of the equation what you do to the other") and were asked to draw the concept.

3. Allow just a few minutes for silent drawing, and then ask students to share their sketches with each other.

4. Monitor sketches for content accuracy and offer feedback when appropriate.

Figure A.4:

Virtual Tug-of-War Debate

Engineered debate enhances student learning in many ways. Emotion increases attention and engagement, aids in memory, and can crystallize thought processes. If debate is carefully engineered, it can make content personally relevant and meaningful to students. In contrast, debate that is dull will have little positive impact. Virtual Tug-of-War Debates add visual stimulus through the use of technology to make discussion more multimodality and engaging.

How to . . .

1. Choose an animation web tool such as www.goanimate.com. Familiarize yourself with its features. Many students will be knowledgeable about these tools and can serve as debate designers.

2. Choose character images to represent both sides of the debate topic. Place the images in an open virtual space, with a rope between them.

3. Insert beginning dialogue for each character, appropriate to your topic, such as, "It is ethical to use animals for drug experimentation because . . ." or "It is unethical to use animals for drug experimentation because . . ."

4. After your basic animation setup is complete, save it for use during the lesson.

5. At the start of the lesson period, assign roles to students. Some will be "pro" and some "con," with three students acting as judges. Assign a student to modify the animation during the debate.

6. Provide the students and the judges with a simple rubric (see Tug-of-War Debate Rubric) for effective debate.

7. Explain to students that they will be debating the topic. They will have a few minutes to work with their teammates to develop arguments. For every point they make that the judges deem valid, a character will be added to their side of the rope in the animation. The winning team is the one that has the most characters to tug on the rope.

Variations . . .

- A similar effect can be achieved without using an animation tool. Open a blank document with your word processing program. Insert two characters with a line or rope strung between them. For each argument made, paste another character into the scene on the corresponding side of the rope.

- Students will love the idea of doing a real tug-of-war. Bring in a one-hundred-foot length of rope. Tie a colorful ribbon in the center of the rope. Take your students outside to an open, grassy area. If a student offers a valid argument for or against the issue, he gets to tie a knot on his side of the rope and stand ready to pull. After all the students have taken sides, mark a line under the center of the rope and begin the tug of war. The game is finished when one team pulls the other team over the center line.

Tug-of-War Debate Rubric

	LEVELS OF PERFORMANCE	
CRITERIA	TRY AGAIN	JOIN YOUR TEAM AND PULL!
Use of Arguments	No reason given or reason is irrelevant to the topic.	Reason is clear and relevant to the topic.
Use of Examples and Facts	No examples or facts.	Example or fact given to support argument.
Use of Rebuttal	No counter-argument offered.	Effective counter-argument speaks directly to other teams' point.
Presentation Style	Tone of voice/gestures are inappropriate (rude, loud, silly, and so on) or not convincing.	Tone of voice and gestures are appropriate and convincing.

WebQuest

A WebQuest is an inquiry-based learning experience that uses Internet technology and focuses on the use of higher-level thinking skills. Students are provided with structured task guidelines, including a variety of prescreened websites. Teachers differentiate the task by choosing websites at various levels of reading and navigation difficulty.

How to . . .

1. WebQuests can be designed using any document with hyperlinks. Tools such as PowerPoint and Prezi add the possibility for interesting visuals, but Word and Excel also work.

2. Choose an interesting task that is related to your content. WebQuests often have a real-life or career application. For example, in a unit on Japanese-American internment camps, a WebQuest might center on causes, comparisons to reactions after the 9/11 bombings, and developing opinions about whether internment camps could happen again. For younger students studying wind energy, a WebQuest might center on the role of engineers in studying wind and inventing applications.

3. Develop a document outlining the specific questions or tasks that students must address. Include hyperlinks to websites that will assist them with the tasks. WebQuests usually do not involve a lot of surfing and searching—instead they are time-efficient ways to use the Internet for information. Consider developing a color code or legend that guides students to more or less complex sites.

4. Websites such as www.webquest.org include numerous shared WebQuests developed by teachers all over the world. These can be used as is, or as models for developing your own WebQuest.

5. Students often work on WebQuests in small groups to encourage collaborative skills. If the WebQuest is designed for group work, be sure to include specific roles and responsibilities for each member so that all students participate fully.

Work Masks

Many students have difficulty processing visual information. A simple solution to this problem is to use Work Masks. Made from file folders, Work Masks cover a portion of a student worksheet or test so that the student can focus on the material needed at the moment.

How to . . .

1. Obtain one file folder for each student.

2. Holding the file vertically, divide the front into thirds and mark these locations with pencil.

3. Using scissors, cut a horizontal line through the front of the folder so that the folder has three flaps.

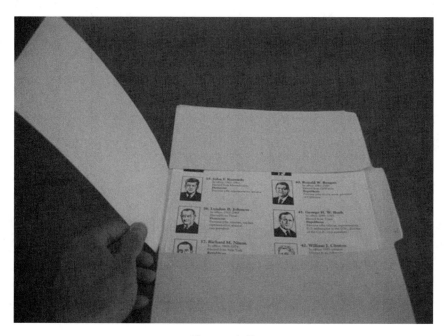

Figure A.5:

4. Show the students how to slide their worksheet or test into the folder, flipping back the top flap so that the top portion of the page is visible.

5. Explain that when they have finished the questions in the visible space, they can close the top flap and open the middle one, and then repeat for the bottom section.

You Lose Bingo

Bingo engages students quickly because of the random possibilities for winning. Random reinforcement has been shown in numerous studies to be more powerful than regular, predictable reinforcement. In You Lose Bingo, students experience the same randomness, but in ways that emphasize loss—loss of control, loss of goods, loss of health—and help students empathize with emotions related to loss.

How to . . .

1. Generate a bingo card template. Bingo cards usually include twenty-five squares arranged in a five-by-five-inch grid, with "Free Space" marked in the center square.

2. Consider your content and develop a list of a minimum of twenty-four things that might be lost as a result of an event or action. In primary grades, You Lose Bingo might be used for a unit on environmental pollution. Losses could include polar bears, clean air, clear mountain views, drinking water, and safe playgrounds. In a secondary level unit on Germany during World War II, a list of things lost by Jews might include a job, home, car, jewelry, food, family members, right to worship, travel, and freedom of speech.

3. For best results, develop twenty-four different variations of the You Lose Bingo card by typing the items into different spaces.

4. For each item that might be lost, develop a corresponding slip of paper to be pulled randomly from a container. The slip should contain an extended explanation of the loss. For example, if the item on the bingo card is "jewelry," the slip of paper might state: "Your grandmother's bracelet, your silver Star of David—even your wedding rings are taken from you."

5. Provide each student with a You Lose Bingo card and bingo chips or pennies to place on the squares. Explain that when a slip is pulled from the box and read aloud, students should scan their card to see if they have that item. If so, they are to

place a chip on the corresponding space. Each time a slip is read aloud, the teacher will say "If you have [name the item], You Lose."

6. As play progresses, stop occasionally to allow students to talk about their losses, share feelings, and make connections.

7. When a student has chips on five items in a row (horizontally, vertically, or diagonally) they are to call out "Bingo!" In traditional bingo, this signifies the end of the game. You Lose Bingo is more effective if time permits you to continue on. By playing beyond the first "loser," all students have an opportunity to experience greater loss and reflect on their simulated experience.

REFERENCES

Allred, T. April, 2010. "Introduction to Climbing." http://www.rockclimbing.com/Articles/Introduction_to_Climbing/Start_Climbing_-_Part_1_Introduction_Overview_1.html.

American Speech-Language-Hearing Association. 2010. *Roles and Responsibilities of Speech-Language Pathologists in Schools.* ASHA: Rockville, MD.

Anderson, M. 2010. *The Well-Balanced Teacher.* Alexandria, VA: Association for Supervision and Curriculum Development.

Archambault, F. A., Jr., Westberg, K. L., Brown, S. W., Hallmark, B. W., Emmons, C. L., and Zhang, W. 1993. *Regular Classroom Practices with Gifted Students: Results of a National Survey of Classroom Teachers* (Research Monograph 93102). Storrs: The National Research Center on the Gifted and Talented, University of Connecticut.

Basso, D., and McCoy, N. 2007. *The Co-Teaching Manual.* Columbia, SC: Twins.

Beninghof, A. 2008. *Engage All Students Through Differentiation.* Peterborough, NH: Crystal Springs.

Beninghof, A. 1998. *SenseAble Strategies.* Longmont, CO: Sopris West.

Beninghof, A., and Singer, A. L. 1995. *Ideas for Inclusion: The School Administrator's Guide.* Longmont, CO: Sopris West.

Bennis, W., and Ward Biederman, P. 1997. *Organizing Genius: The Secrets of Creative Collaboration.* New York: Perseus Books.

Bowen-Irish, T. 2010. "Collaboration and the Curriculum." *Advance for Occupational Therapy Practitioners* 26(9): 35.

Burns, T. March 2010. "Co-Teaching at Merry Acres Middle School." Presented at the Association for Supervision and *Curriculum Development Annual Conference*, San Antonio.

Carbo, M. 1994. *Reading Style Inventory.* Syosset, NY: National Reading Styles Institute.

Carbo, M. 2009. "Match the Style of Instruction to the Style of Reading." *Phi Delta Kappan* 90(5): 373–378.

Chauncey, C. 2005. *Recruiting, Retaining, and Supporting Highly Qualified Teachers*. Cambridge: Harvard Education Press.

Division for Learning Disabilities of the Council for Exceptional Children (DLD CEC). 2001. "A Focus on Co-Teaching." *Current Practice Alert Issue 6*, Autumn.

Denton, P. 2008. "The Power of Our Words." *Educational Leadership* 66(1): 28–31.

Dieker, L. 2001. "What Are the Characteristics of 'Effective' Middle and High School Co-Taught Teams?" *Preventing School Failure* 46(1): 14–23.

Dieker, L., and Murawski, W. 2003. "Co-Teaching at the Secondary Level: Unique Issues, Current Trends and Suggestions for Success." *The High School Journal* 86(4): 1–13.

Dunn, R., and Dunn, K. 1993. *Teaching Secondary Students Through Their Individual Learning Styles*. Boston: Allyn & Bacon, 1993.

Dunn, R., Dunn, K., and Price, G. 1994. *Learning Style Inventory*. Lawrence, KS: Price Systems.

Fattig, M., and Taylor, M. 2008. *Co-Teaching in the Differentiated Classroom*. San Francisco: Jossey-Bass.

Ferlazzo, L. 2010. *English Language Learners: Teaching Strategies That Work*. Santa Barbara: ABC-CLIO.

Fredricks, J., Blumenthal, P. and Paris, A. (2004). "School Engagement: Potential of the Concept: State of the Evidence." *Review of Educational Research*, 74: 59–119.

Fredricks, J., McColskey, W., Meli, J., Mordica, J., Montrosse, B., and Mooney, K. 2011. "Measuring Student Engagement in Upper Elementary Through High School: a Description of 21 Instruments." (Issues & Answers Report, REL 2011–No. 098). Washington, DC: U.S. Department of Education, Institute of Education Sciences, National Center for Education Evaluation and Regional Assistance, Regional Educational Laboratory Southeast. Retrieved from http://ies.ed.gov/ncee/edlabs.

Freiberg, H. J. 1998. "Measuring School Climate: Let Me Count the Ways." *Educational Leadership* 56(1): 22–26.

Fullan, M. 2007 *The New Meaning of Educational Change*. New York: Teachers College Press.

Garan, E., and DeVoogd, G. 2008. "The Benefits of Sustained Silent Reading: Scientific Research and Common Sense Converge." *Reading Teacher* 62(4): 336–344.

Gardner, H. 1997. Remarks made at the 69th Annual International Conference for the Association for Supervision and Curriculum Development, Baltimore, MD.

Gardner, H. 1993. *Multiple Intelligences: The Theory in Practice*. New York: Basic Books.

Gay, G. 2000. *Culturally Responsive Teaching*. New York: Teachers College Press.

Gostick, A., and Elton, C. 2010. *The Orange Revolution: How One Great Team Can Transform an Entire Organization*. New York: Free Press.

Gurian, M., and Stevens, K. 2005. *The Minds of Boys: Saving Our Sons from Falling Behind in School and Life*. San Francisco: Jossey-Bass.

Hadley, P., Simmerman, A., Long, M., and Luna, M. 2000. "Facilitating Language Development for Inner-City Children: Experimental Evaluation of a Collaborative, Classroom-Based Intervention." *Language, Speech and Hearing Services in Schools, 31*: 280–295.

Hargreaves, A., and Shirley, D. 2009. *The Fourth Way: The Inspiring Future for Educational Change*. Thousand Oaks, CA: Corwin.

Haynes, J. 2007. *Getting Started with English Language Learners*. Alexandria, VA: Association for Supervision and Curriculum Development.

Heath, C., and Heath, D. 2010. *Switch: How to Change Things When Change Is Hard*. New York: Broadway Books.

Hill, J., and Flynn, K. 2006. *Classroom Instruction That Works for English Language Learners*. Alexandria, VA: Association for Supervision and Curriculum Development.

Hodgin, J., and Wooliscroft, C. 1997. "Eric Learns to Read: Learning Styles at Work." *Educational Leadership* 54(6): 43–45.

Hollins, E. 2006. "Transforming Practice in Urban Schools." *Educational Leadership* 63(6): 48.

Honigsfeld, A., and Dove, M. 2010. *Collaboration and Co-Teaching: Strategies for English Learners*. Thousand Oaks, CA: Corwin.

Hunt, P., Goetz, L., and Anderson, J. 1986. "The Quality of IEP Objectives Associated with Placement on Integrated Versus Segregated School Sites." *Journal of the Association for Persons with Severe Handicaps 11*(2): 125–30.

International Reading Association (IRA). *Teaching All Children to Read: The Roles of the Reading Specialist: A Position Statement of the International Reading Association.* 2000, 1–5.

Johnson, S. 2010. *Where Good Ideas Come From: The Natural History of Innovation.* New York: Penguin.

Kagan, S., and Kagan, M. 2008. *Kagan Cooperative Learning.* San Clemente, CA: Kagan.

L'Allier, S., Elish-Piper, L., and Bean, R. 2010. "What Matters for Elementary Literacy Coaching? Guiding Principles for Instructional Improvement and Student Achievement." *The Reading Teacher, 63*(7): 544–554.

Maiers, A. *Seedlings Show 104.* http://edtechtalk.com/node/4898. Feb. 2011.

Marzano, R. 2010. *Formative Assessment and Standards-Based Grading.* Bloomington, IN: Marzano Research Laboratory.

Marzano, R., and Pickering, D. 2010. *The Highly Engaged Classroom.* Bloomington, IN: Marzano Research Laboratory.

Maxwell, J. C. 2010. *Everyone Communicates, Few Connect.* Nashville: Nelson.

McCarthy, B. 1996. *About Learning.* Barrington, IL: Excel.

Mendez-Morse, S. 1992. *Leadership Characteristics that Facilitate School Change.* Austin, TX: SEDL.

Murawski, W. 2009. *Collaborative Teaching in Secondary Schools.* Thousand Oaks, CA: Corwin.

Murawski, W. 2008. "Five Keys to Co-Teaching in Inclusive Classrooms." *The School Administrator, 27.*

Murawski, W., and Dieker, L. 2008. "50 Ways to Keep Your Co-Teacher." *Teaching Exceptional Children 40*(4): 40–48.

Murawski, W., and Swanson, H. 2001. "A Meta-Analysis of Co-Teaching Research: Where Are the Data?" *Remedial and Special Education 22*(5): 258–267.

National Association for Gifted Children. 1993. *Collaboration Between Gifted and General Education Programs*. NAGC: Washington, D.C.

Painter, B., and Valentine, J. 1996. *The Instructional Practices Inventory*. Middle Level Leadership Center. http://www.MLLC.org.

Pink, D. 2009. *Drive: The Surprising Truth About What Motivates Us*. New York: Riverhead.

Pittsford Central School District. 2006. High School Student Co-Teaching Survey Data. Pittsford, NY. (unpublished)

Popham, W. J. 2008. *Transformative Assessment*. Alexandria, VA: Association for Supervision and Curriculum Development.

Ratey, J. 2008. *Spark: The Revolutionary New Science of Exercise and the Brain*. New York: Little Brown.

Robinson, K. 2006. *How Schools Are Killing Creativity*. TED Talks. http://www.ted.com/talks/ken_robinson_says_schools_kill_creativity.html.

Sapon-Shevin, M. 2008. "Learning in an Inclusive Community." *Educational Leadership*, 66(1): 49–53.

Schmoker, M., 2001. "The Crayola Curriculum." *Education Week*, October 24.

Santa, C., Havens, L., & Valdes. B. 2004. *Project CRISS: Creating Independence Through Student-Owned Strategies*. Dubuque, IA: Kendall-Hunt.

Scott, S. 2004. *Fierce Conversations: Achieving Success at Work and in Life, One Conversation at a Time*. New York: Berkeley Books.

Scruggs, T., Mastropieri, M., & McDuff, P. 2007. "Co-Teaching in Inclusive Classrooms: A Metasynthesis of Qualitative Research." *Exceptional Children*, 7, June.

Silver, H., Strong, R., and Perini, M. 2007. *The Strategic Teacher*. Alexandria, VA: Association for Supervision and Curriculum Development.

Sprenger, M. 2005. *How to Teach So Students Remember*. Alexandria, VA: Association for Supervision and Curriculum Development.

Stiggins, R., Arter, J., Chappuis, J., and Chappuis, S. 2006. *Classroom Assessment for Student Learning*. Princeton, NJ: Merrill Prentice Hall.

Tapscott, D. 2009. *Grown Up Digital*. New York: McGraw-Hill.

Theoharis, G., and Causton-Theoharis, J. 2010. "Include, Belong, Learn." *Educational Leadership* 68(2). http://www.ascd.org/publications/educational-leadership/oct10/vol68/num02/Include,-Belong,-Learn.aspx.

Throneburg, R., and others. 2000. "A Comparison of Service Delivery Models: Effects on Curricular Vocabulary Skills in the School Setting." *American Journal of Speech-Language Pathology*, 9: 10–20.

Tomlinson, C. 1999. *The Differentiated Classroom: Responding to the Needs of All Learners*. Alexandria, VA: Association for Supervision and Curriculum Development.

Tuckman, B. 1965. "Developmental Sequence in Small Groups." *Psychological Bulletin*, 63(6): 384–399.

Villa, R., Thousand, J., and Nevin, A. 2004. *A Guide to Co-Teaching: Practical Tips for Facilitating Student Learning*. Thousand Oaks, CA: Corwin.

Wiggins, G., and McTighe, J. 2006. "Examining the Teaching Life." *Educational Leadership*, 63(6).

Willingham, D. 2009. *Why Don't Students Like School?* San Francisco: Jossey-Bass.

Willis, J. 2008. *What Today's Neuroscience Might Mean for the Classrooms of Tomorrow*. ASCD Annual Conference. New Orleans: Association for Supervision and Curriculum Development.

Wolfensberger, W. 1983, "Social Role Valorisation: A Proposed New Term for the Principle of Normalisation." *Mental Retardation*, 21: 234–239.

INDEX

Page references followed by *w* indicate a worksheet; followed by *e* indicate an exhibit; followed by *t* indicate a table.

general education/special education teams using, 144; guiding questions when considering the, 62; as most beneficial to students, 55; Parallel Teaching Model inclusion as component of, 56, 57*t*, 108; pros and cons of the, 52*t*, 60–62; Skill Groups Model inclusion as component of, 81; summing up the, 62; synopsis of, 52*t*; unit plan using, 56, 57*t*, 58

Dunn, K., 95, 96, 97

Dunn, R., 95, 96, 97

E

Education: need to individualize, 95; slow process of change in, 16. *See also* General education; Special education

Educators: co-teaching definitions from survey of, 8; types involved in co-teaching relationships, 7. *See also* Specialists; Teachers

El (English Learner) student, 188

Elish-Piper, L., 185

ELL (English Language Learner) specialists: co-teaching with, 61, 187–193; Speak and Add Model issues for, 76; Station Teaching Model applications by, 87, 88; tool it items used by, 190

Elton, C., 21

English 10 "Night" by Elie Wiesel (lesson plan), 146*e*

Equal treatment, 18–19

ESL (English as a Secondary Language) specialists, 188

Evaluation: Co-Teaching Observation Tool worksheet for, 45, 47*w*; importance of including teachers in, 42, 45; Instructional Practices Inventory used for, 45, 48*t*–49*t*; Parent Survey worksheet for, 42, 44*w*; Speak and Add Model approach to, 74; Student Survey worksheet for, 42, 43*w*; Teacher Survey worksheet for, 45, 46*w*; valuation data gathered through, 42. *See also* Assessment

Everyone Communicates, Few Connect (Maxwell), 17

"Examining the Teaching Life" (Wiggins and McTighe), 25

Exhibits: Additional Tasks Checklist, 30, 32*e*; Co-Taught Lesson with an SLP, 155*e*; Co-Teaching Grading Questions, 40, 41*e*; Co-Teaching Models Checklist, 24*e*;

Co-Teaching Responsibility Checklist, 30, 31*e*; English 10 "Night" by Elie Wiesel, 146*e*; Reflective Questions for Co-Teaching Teams, 26*e*; Test Design and Adaptation, 117*e*

Expanded standards: Colorado Department of Education, Expanded Standards, 125*t*; Complementary Skills Model use to teach, 53*t*, 57*t*, 58, 123–130; definition of, 124

F

Faculty. *See* Teachers

Fair treatment, 18–19

Fast-tracking co-team teaching, 197–198

Ferlazzo, L., 192

504 plans: accommodations agreements in, 89, 114–115; Adapting Model benefits of ensuring commitments of, 120

Flexible schedules ("flex time"), 38

Flynn, K., 188

Forest, M., 16

Formative assessment: definition of, 65; Lead and Support Model use of, 65–66

Forming stage of co-teaching, 25

Fredericks, J., 45

Freiberg, H. J., 17

Friend, M., 16

Fullan, M., 17

G

Garan, E., 38

Gardner, H., 95, 96

Gay, G., 191

General Co-Teaching Practices Worksheet, 23*w*

General education: Complementary Skills Model focus on teaching skills of, 124; Lead and Support Model benefits to, 64, 68; simile on marriage of special education and, 15–16. *See also* Education; Special education

General education/ELL specialist teams: benefits of using, 61, 187–188; best models to use for, 188–190; challenges facing, 191; discussion questions on, 193; ELL's tool kit items used for, 190; essential for success, 192–193; lesson plan for, 189*t*; summing up, 193

General education/gifted specialists team: benefits for students, 174–715; best models

Pink, D., 39

Pittsford Central School District, 11, 12

PL 94-142, 16

Planning time: additional strategies to create, 38–39; co-teaching with paraeducator, 169–170; general education/technology specialist's, 138; Lead and Support Model advantages for, 68; long-range solutions for creating, 39–40; obtaining grants to pay stipends for, 40; process of developing good ideas during available, 36–37; "serendipitous," 39; Speak and Add Model requiring little, 74; sustained silent reading (SSR) to create, 38; ways to utilize substitute teachers to create, 37–38

Poor communication: co-teaching derailed by, 21; rockclimbing and price of, 21

Popham, W. J., 65

Prairie Crossing Elementary School (Colorado), 138

Prep period, 37

Price, G., 97

Principle of natural proportions, 157

Problem solving standards (Colorado Department of Education), 125t

Professional goals, 21–22

Professional growth: co-teaching benefits for, 10; Duet Model benefits for, 61; SLP's co-teaching success and potential for, 157

R

Ratey, J., 145

Readiness levels, 83

Reading Style Inventory, 97

Reflective Questions for Co-Teaching Teams, 26e

"Related services," 160

Relationships. See Co-teaching relationships

Respect: for individual differences, 18; interactions mindful of, 19

Response to Intervention (RtI), 152

Responsibilities. See Co-teaching roles/responsibilities

Responsive Classrooms, 19

Richert, C., 178

"Roaming Sub Strategy," 37

Robinson, Sir K., 19

Rockclimbing communication, 20–21

Rockclimbing.com, 20

S

Sapon-Shevin, M., 17, 18

Schmoker, M., 103

School districts: Douglas County School District (Denver), 134; grading policies and procedures of, 40; Jefferson County Public Schools (Colorado), 189; Papillion LaVista School District (Nebraska), 152; substitute teaching policies and procedures of, 37–39

Schools: Huber Heights City Schools (Ohio), 182; Prairie Crossing Elementary School (Colorado), 138; technology as part of master schedule, 137–138

Scruggs, T., 9

Self advocacy/self determination skills, 125t

Sense of belonging, 13

"Serendipitous" planning times, 39

Shirley, D., 17

Silver, H., 96

Simmerman, A., 9

Simultaneous engagement, 8

Singer, A. L., 30

Skill Groups Model: at a glance description of, 79–81; Collaborative Teaching Responsibilities Checklist—Skill Groups, 81, 82t; Duet Model unit plan inclusion of, 56, 57t, 58; general education/gifted specialist team using, 175; general education/literacy specialist team using, 182; general education/OT or PT teams using, 160; general education/special education teams using, 144; guiding questions when considering the, 84; lesson plan using the, 80t; pros and cons of, 52t, 83–84; used as Skill Groups Model component, 81; summing up the, 85; synopsis of, 52t

"The slow hunch," 37

Small groups: avoiding sense of tracking when working with, 84; Skill Groups Model use of, 83–84; Station Model use of, 88–90. See also Groups

Speak and Add Model: at a glance description of, 71–74; Collaborative Teaching Responsibilities Checklist—Speak and Add, 74, 75t; Duet Model unit plan inclusion of, 56, 57t; examples of co-teaching applications of, 73t; general education/ELL teams using, 190; general education/literacy specialist team using, 182–183; general education/special education teams using, 145; general education/

technology specialists teams using, 135; guiding questions when considering the, 77; "jump-in" permission importance during, 71; paraeducator use of, 167–168; pros and cons of, 52t, 74, 76–77; summing up the, 77; synopsis of, 52t

Special education: IDEA (Individuals with Disabilities Education Act) on, 16, 143, 151, 160; PL 94-142 mandate on, 16; smilie on marriage between general education and, 15–16. *See also* Education; General education

Special education students: classroom composition which includes, 148; creating sense of belonging in, 13; paraeducator working with autistic, 167–168; providing "related services" to, 160; Response to Intervention (RtI) for struggling, 152; rising to higher expectations, 13; Speak and Add Model approach to struggling, 73; testing accommodations for, 89–90. *See also* Accommodations; IEPs (Individualized Education Plans); Students; Targeted students

Special educators: general education teacher co-teaching with, 141–150; limiting co-teaching partnerships of, 148; research on co-teaching with, 9

Specialists: benefits of co-teaching with ELL, 61; bringing them in to teach on occasion, 38, 62; co-teaching with a technology, 133–139; definition of, 51; Duet Model benefits for professional growth of, 61; ELL (English Language Learner), 61, 76, 87, 88, 187–193; ESL (English as a Secondary Language), 188; gifted, 173–179; Lead and Support Model use of, 64, 65–66; literacy, 181–186; modifications overseen by, 116; occupational or physical therapist (OT/PT), 159–164; paraeducators, 38, 165–171; Skill Groups Model roles of, 81, 82t; Speak and Add Model issues for ELL, 76; special educators, 9, 141–150; speech/language pathologists (SLPs), 151–158. *See also* Educators; Teachers

Speech and Language Pathologists (SLPs): co-teaching with, 153–158; description of services by, 151; "old rules" vs. "new rules" for, 151–153

Sprenger, M., 90

Standardized testing: accommodations for, 89–90, 116, 117e, 118; co-teaching research on outcomes of, 9

Station Teaching Model: at a glance description of, 87–90; Collaborative Teaching

Responsibilities Checklist—Station Teaching, 90, 91t; general education/OT or PT teams using, 160; guiding questions when considering, 92; pros and cons of, 52t, 90, 92; speech/language pathologists (SLPs) use of, 154, 156; summing up the, 93; synopsis of, 52t

Stiggins, R., 66

Storming stage of co-teaching, 25

Strategic adaptation tools, 115

Strong, R., 96

Student engagement: changing vocal qualities, teaching styles, and personalities used for, 76; expectations for contributions and, 19–20; gathering evaluation data on, 45; how co-teaching increases, 11–12; Reflective Questions for Co-Teaching Teams on, 26e

Student learning: access skills, 53t, 57t, 58, 123–130; co-teaching research on, 9–10; Colorado Department of Education, Expanded Standards on, 125t; language skills, 9, 61, 87–193; literacy achievement, 9, 181–186; rising to higher expectations, 13; sustained silent reading (SSR) outcomes for, 38; vocabulary acquisition, 9

Student Learning Style Observation Tool worksheet, 97, 98w

Student Survey worksheet, 42, 43w

Students: cluster grouping of, 35–36; co-teaching and behavior management of, 11; co-teaching support for unidentified, 12; creating a comprehensive learning profile of, 97; as digital natives, 134; El (English Learner), 188; encouraging independence of, 20; expecting contributions from all, 19–20; fair versus equal treatment of, 18–19; gifted, 174–179; increasing teacher access by, 11; LEP (Limited English Proficiency), 188; Student Survey for evaluation data from, 42, 43w. *See also* Accommodations; Special education students; Targeted students

Students with disabilities. *See* Special education students

Style differences, 22

Substitute teachers: to cover during IEP meetings, 37–38; hiring a rotating long-term, 39; put to work during the prep period, 37; "Roaming Sub Strategy" for using, 37; specialists used as occasional, 38, 62

Summative assessment, 89–90

Supervision of paraeducators, 169
Sustained silent reading (SSR), 38
Swanson, H., 9

T

Tactile instruction modality: differentiated assessment activities and tools, 101t; ELL specialists' incorporation of, 192; general education/special education team use of, 145; Learning Style Model lesson plans using, 99, 100fig; OT/PT use of, 161; sharing responsibility to use, 101, 102t

Tapscott, D., 134

Targeted students: Adapting Model expectations for accommodating, 113–121; creating a comprehensive learning profile of, 97; definition of, 51; EI (English Learner), 188; formative assessment of, 65–66; gifted, 174–179; LEP (Limited English Proficiency), 188; Skill Groups Model use of whole group/small groups of, 83–84; Speak and Add Model advantages for, 76; Station Teaching Model's focused approach to, 87–90, 92; summative assessment of, 89–90. See also Accommodations; Special education students; Students

Teacher Survey worksheet, 45, 46w

Teachers: building bridges between, 18; co-teaching facilitating professional growth of, 10; co-teaching as increasing access to, 11; co-teaching for simultaneous engagement in instruction, 8; confusion about paraeducator supervision by, 169; as digital immigrants, 134; substitute, 37–38, 39, 62; Teacher Survey worksheet for evaluation data from, 45, 46w; who embrace inclusion, 148. See also Co-teachers; Educators; Specialists

Teaching goals, 21

Teaching philosophy, 21

Teaching styles: of individual co-teachers, 22; student engagement through changes in, 76

Technology: included into school's master schedule, 137–138; teaching skills related to, 125t

Technology specialists. See General education/technology specialists teams

TED Talk, 19

Teen suicide, 13

Testing accommodations: Adapting Model approach to, 116, 117e, 118; during

summative assessment, 89–90; Test Design and Adaptation for, 117e

Theoharis, G., 9

Think-Pair-Timed Share, 192

Thousand, J., 8, 39

Throneburg, R., 9

Time on task, 12

Tomlinson, C. A., 68, 144

Tuckman, B., 25

U

Unidentified students, 12

Unit plans (Duet Model), 56, 57t, 58. See also Lesson plans

U.S. Department of Education, 187

V

Valentine, J., 45, 49

Villa, R., 8, 16, 39

Vision statement: on embracing collaborative relationships, 17; including independence as part of, 20

Visual instruction modality: differentiated assessment activities and tools, 101t; ELL specialists' incorporation of, 192; Learning Style Model lesson plans using, 99, 100t; sharing responsibility to use, 101, 102t

Vocabulary acquisition, 9

W

Weber, M., 189

The Well-Balanced Teacher (Anderson), 30, 33

Where Good Ideas Come From (Johnson), 10, 36–37

Whole-group approach: Parallel Teaching Model use of, 105, 108; Skill Groups Model use of, 83

Wiesel, E., 145, 146e

Wiggins, G., 25

Willis, J., 145

Wolfensberger, W., 165

Wooliscraft, C., 145

Worksheets: General Co-Teaching Practices Worksheet, 23w; Parent Survey, 42, 44w; Student Learning Style Observation Tool, 97, 98w; Student Survey, 42, 43w